SPECTRUM
Science
Test Practice

Grade 4

Published by Spectrum
an imprint of Carson-Dellosa Publishing LLC
Greensboro, NC

Spectrum
An imprint of Carson-Dellosa Publishing LLC
P.O. Box 35665
Greensboro, NC 27425 USA

Printed in Mayfield, PA U.S.A. • All rights reserved.   ISBN 0-7696-8064-X

4 5 6 7 8 9 10 1 PAH 14 13 12 11 10

SCIENCE TEST PRACTICE
Table of Contents
Grade 4

Science Test Practice is for everyone who wants to have a working knowledge of the fundamentals of science. Written with the goal of helping students achieve on science tests, it approaches science through the format of the National Science Education Standards.

The National Science Education Standards were developed by the National Academy of Science, an organization of the leading scientists in the United States. Their goal is for all students to achieve scientific literacy. To be scientifically literate means to be able to understand the richness of the world around us; to be able to make decisions based on the skills and processes that science teaches us; and to approach problems and challenges creatively.

This book is divided into sections, each one based on a National Science Education Content Standard. Through the Pretest, you will see where the student's strengths and challenges lie. Then the students will be exposed to each content area through the course of the book. Finally, a Posttest will show you and the student how far he or she has come!

Each section begins with a brief description of the Content Standard covered within. This book focuses on content standards A–D: science inquiry, physical science, life science, and earth/space science. The remaining content standards, which cover science and technology and science in personal and social perspectives, are covered within the book. A correlation chart details the coverage of all standards in the book (see pp. 7–8).

Students can begin with the Pretest (pp. 9–14). This test covers all the three major strands of science:

- physical science, which includes how objects move and interact;

- life science, which includes animals, plants, and ecosystems;

- earth and space science, which includes rocks and minerals, the oceans, and the solar system.

After the Pretest, you may wish to complete the test prep practice in order, or complete the sections out of sequence. Although they are not labeled as such, the pages generally deal with specific topics within the field—for example, ecosystems or the rock cycle.

Finally, the Posttest gives the student a chance to practice yet again, applying the knowledge gleaned from the rest of the book. A complete answer key appears at the back of the book.

With its real-life questions and standards-based approach, *Science Test Practice* will engage students, give them solid test-taking hints and practice, and provide them with an opportunity to build their confidence for other exams.

0-7696-8064-X—*Science Test Practice*

National Science Education Content Standards Correlation

Each national content standard begins with the phrase, "As a result of activities in grades K–4, all students should develop . . ."

Standard	Pages
CONTENT STANDARD A: Science as Inquiry	
Abilities necessary to do scientific inquiry	9, 12, 14, 16–18, 22, 24, 68, 88, 91
To learn about the world in a scientific manner, students need to learn how to ask questions, formulate possible answers, devise ways of testing those answers, and base their conclusions on evidence.	
Understanding about scientific inquiry	10, 16–18, 19–24, 46, 48–50, 52, 68, 74, 77, 88–89, 91
Students need to understand that the investigations used to gather information depend on the question being asked; that scientists use mathematics and technology as they work; and that scientists build on the work other scientists have done, by asking questions about that work and that grow out of that work.	
CONTENT STANDARD B: Physical Science	
Properties of objects and materials	9–10, 22, 26–32, 34–35, 89–91
Position and motion of objects	10–12 27 30 35 36 40 41 42
Light, heat, electricity, and magnetism	9, 13, 16–17, 23, 31, 33–39, 43–44 89
CONTENT STANDARD C: Life Science	
The characteristics of organisms	9, 12, 18, 20, 46–48, 50, 52–55, 58, 62–65, 89
Life cycles of organisms	9, 51, 54–55, 59, 66
Organisms and environments	9, 48–50, 52–56–57, 59–66, 68, 90
CONTENT STANDARD D: Earth and Space Science	
Properties of Earth materials	9, 11–13, 68–72, 74–77, 81–82, 88–89
Objects in the sky	10, 12, 42, 76–79, 85–87, 89
Changes in Earth and sky	12, 14, 72–75, 78, 81, 85–87, 90

0-7696-8064-X—*Science Test Practice*

National Science Education Content Standards Correlation

CONTENT STANDARD E: Science and Technology	
Abilities of technological design	9, 19, 43–44, 89
Understanding about science and technology	10, 19, 23–24, 89
Abilities to distinguish between natural objects and objects made by humans	11, 19, 89
CONTENT STANDARD F: Science in Personal and Social Perspectives	
Science can seem removed from everyday life, but it actually surrounds us. Personal hygiene activities are based in scientific reasoning. Understanding the risks and benefits in the world makes students more informed citizens.	
Personal health	12, 23, 88–90
Characteristics and changes in populations	56–57, 65, 90
Types of resources	68, 72, 76, 83, 88, 90
Changes in environments	68, 76, 83, 88, 90
Science and technology in local challenges	68, 71, 76, 81
CONTENT STANDARD G: History and Nature of Science	
Science as a human endeavor	9–14, 16–17, 20–21, 27, 39, 66, 88–91
Science is a pursuit of human beings, with many different skills, backgrounds, qualities, and talents. However, scientists all share curiosity about the world, a tendency to ask questions about what is known, an openness to new ideas, insight, and creativity.	

0-7696-8064-X— *Science Test Practice*

Name_____ Date_____

Grade 4 Pretest

Directions: Read the questions. Choose the truest possible answer. Shade in the circle before your choice.

HINT: Read the question before you look at the answers.

1. **Rosa is using a thermometer to measure the temperature of a cup of tea. What is she really measuring?**
   - (A) the tea particles' density
   - (B) the tea particles' buoyancy
   - (C) the tea particles' energy of motion
   - (D) the tea particles' pressure

2. **Jamal touches the outside of a cold glass of water. In which direction does the heat move?**
   - (F) from the glass to the water
   - (G) from the water to the glass
   - (H) from Jamal's hand to the glass
   - (J) from the glass to Jamal's hand

3. **A farmer plants wheat on the same patch of soil every year. How will this affect the soil?**
   - (A) It will erode the soil, which will weaken the wheat crop.
   - (B) It will make sure that there is plenty of nitrogen to feed the crops.
   - (C) It will lead to nutrient loss, which will make it harder for wheat to grow.
   - (D) It will cause the land to produce more nutrients in order to adapt to the wheat.

4. **How do most plants or animals become fossils?**
   - (F) They are buried under volcanic ash.
   - (G) They are preserved under rivers and lakes.
   - (H) They are buried by sediments after they die.
   - (J) They are swallowed whole by a larger animal.

5. **When Felipe tosses a ball into a pail of water, it floats. This shows him that the ball must be _____ .**
   - (A) hollow
   - (B) made of plastic
   - (C) perfectly round
   - (D) less dense than water

6. **The viceroy butterfly has the same pattern on its wings as the monarch butterfly. Because birds do not like the taste of the monarch butterfly, they will avoid a viceroy butterfly, too. What is this an example of?**
   - (F) mimicry
   - (G) instinct
   - (H) migration
   - (J) camouflage

0-7696-8064-X—*Science Test Practice*

Name_____ Date_____

Directions: Study the diagram to the right. Use it to help you answer question 7.

7. Arielle is pushing against one side of a box with 10 N of force. Bashir is pushing against the other side of the box using 10 N of force. What will happen to the box?

    Ⓐ It will move upwards.

    Ⓑ It will not move at all.

    Ⓒ It will move toward Arielle.

    Ⓓ It will move towards Bashir.

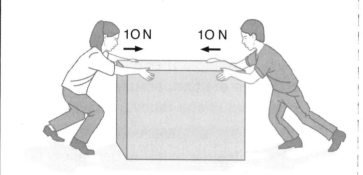

Directions: Read the questions. Choose the truest possible answer. Shade in the circle before your choice.

8. Sometimes matter changes its state. In which of the following events will this happen?

    Ⓕ Matt eats a bowl of soup.

    Ⓖ Yoshi's mother lights a match.

    Ⓗ Susie mixes together two different types of sand.

    Ⓙ Tanisha puts a glass of orange juice in the freezer.

9. When Adam goes outside in the summertime, he feels the sun beating down on him. What is he really feeling?

    Ⓐ waste heat

    Ⓑ solar convection

    Ⓒ infrared radiation

    Ⓓ convection currents

10. What forms when a cold air mass meets a warm air mass?

    Ⓕ a cold front

    Ⓖ a warm front

    Ⓗ a cirrus cloud

    Ⓙ a cumulus cloud

11. Rivka wants to fit her little brother's blocks into a box, so she is measuring the box. Which feature of the box should she measure?

    Ⓐ mass

    Ⓑ weight

    Ⓒ volume

    Ⓓ density

GO ON

Name _____   Date _____

Directions: Read the questions. Choose the truest possible answer. Shade in the circle before your choice.

HINT: Cross out answer choices you know are wrong to help you find the correct answer.

12. **Sandstone is a soft rock that is made of grains of sand that are stuck together. What type of rock is sandstone?**
    - (A) igneous
    - (B) volcanic
    - (C) metamorphic
    - (D) sedimentary

13. **Erica walked from her house to Lola's house in ten minutes. To figure out her speed, what other piece of information would she have to know?**
    - (F) the force of gravity
    - (G) Erica's mass and volume
    - (H) the length of Erica's steps
    - (J) the distance to Lola's house

14. **What causes tides?**
    - (A) gravity
    - (B) wind
    - (C) fault lines
    - (D) density of water

15. **The particles in which state of matter move most slowly?**
    - (F) gas
    - (G) solid
    - (H) vapor
    - (J) liquid

16. **Rebecca wants to measure the wind's speed. Which instrument should she use?**
    - (A) wind sock
    - (B) barometer
    - (C) speedometer
    - (D) anemometer

17. **Lichen grows on the outside of a rock and slowly breaks the rock down. What is this process called?**
    - (F) erosion
    - (G) weathering
    - (H) conservation
    - (J) photosynthesis

18. **Soil that is dark and spongy probably contains a lot of _____ .**
    - (A) silt
    - (B) clay
    - (C) sand
    - (D) humus

GO ON

0-7696-8064-X—*Science Test Practice*

Grade 4 Pretest

Directions: Read each question. Write your answers on the lines provided.

19. **What is the difference between magma and lava?**

_____

_____

_____

20. **List the four gas giants in the solar system.**

_____

_____

_____

21. **Why do you weigh more on the earth than you would on Pluto?**

_____

_____

_____

22. **What are five basic needs that all living things share?**

_____

_____

_____

23. **How can ways to conserve soil, like contour plowing, strip cropping, and terracing, help farms?**

_____

_____

_____

GO ON

0-7696-8064-X—*Science Test Practice*

Directions: Study the diagram to the right. Use it to help you answer question 24.

24. **Which layer of Earth is the hottest?**

    Ⓐ crust

    Ⓑ mantle

    Ⓒ inner core

    Ⓓ outer core

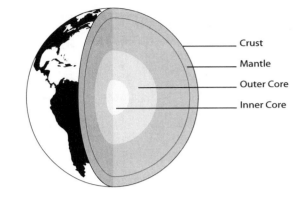

Crust
Mantle
Outer Core
Inner Core

Directions: Study the diagram below. Use it to help you answer questions 25–26.

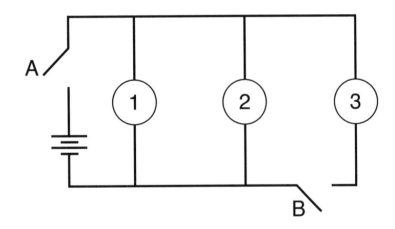

25. **What kind of circuit is this? Why do you think this? Back up your answer with facts.**

_____

_____

_____

26. **Which lights would turn on if Switch A would close but Switch B would remain open?**

_____

_____

_____

GO ON

0-7696-8064-X—*Science Test Practice*

Grade 4 Pretest

Directions: Study the diagram below. Use it to help you answer questions 27–28.

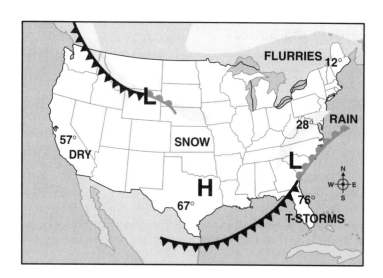

27. **Will plans to go on a picnic tomorrow. He lives in Florida. What would you advise him to do? Why?**

    _____

    _____

    _____

    _____

    _____

28. **Where would you have to wear a heavy winter coat?**

    Ⓐ northeast coast

    Ⓑ southwest coast

    Ⓒ northwest coast

    Ⓓ southeast coast

Directions: Read the question. Write your answer on the lines provided.

29. **What is the greenhouse effect?**

    _____

    _____

    _____

    _____

HINT: When you finish a test, go back and look over your work.

STOP

Content Standard A

The purpose of the first part of the National Science Education Standards is twofold: to give students an understanding of the principles, concepts, and processes that are part of all scientific endeavors, and to build the abilities and skills that are necessary to act as scientists themselves.

Children are natural scientists. The question 'why?' that so often drives parents to distraction, is really the essence of science summed up in a single word. Science is a process of asking questions, thinking of explanations, testing ideas, and either supporting or discarding those ideas, based on the evidence collected.

This section of *Science Test Practice* will give students experience in using scientific tools, including a balance and a thermometer, in thinking critically, and in drawing conclusions based on evidence.

═══════════════════ **Grade 4** ═══════════════════

Directions: Read the text below. Use information from it to help you answer the questions on page 17.

HINT: Read the questions before you read the passage. Look for information as you read that can help you answer the questions.

Ben and the Lightning

Once upon a time, there lived a man named Ben. Ever since childhood, Ben had been interested in everything.

Ben was a newspaper editor, and he published many notices of people who had died when hit by lightning. Lightning also struck homes and other buildings and made them burn down. People in Ben's time were frightened of lightning, but they did not understand what it was. Like many people before them, they were superstitious and thought that lightning only struck someone who had done wrong. However, there was a flaw in their thinking: lightning could strike anyone, not just bad people.

Ben suspected that lightning had a scientific reason. His idea was that lightning was a natural form of electricity. To prove his idea, he devised an experiment.

Metal, Ben knew, would conduct electricity. If he could get a tall metal pole to reach into the sky, it might attract lightning. But perhaps there was an easier way: perhaps he could get a smaller piece of metal up into the sky.

Ben took a child's toy-a kite-and tied a metal key to the string. When a storm came, he went out into the wind and rain and launched the kite. At first, nothing seemed to happen. But before giving up, Ben touched the key. Electricity leaped from the key to his fingertip! Ben had discovered that lightning really was electricity.

You might have heard of Ben. His full name was Benjamin Franklin.

0-7696-8064-X—*Science Test Practice*

Grade 4

Directions: Read each question. Write your answers on the lines provided.

1. What did the people of Ben's time think that lightning was?

_____

_____

_____

2. What question do you think Ben asked about lightning?

_____

_____

_____

3. Below, write a paragraph comparing how Ben thought about lightning and how other people of the time thought about lightning.

_____

_____

_____

_____

_____

4. Below, write a letter to Ben Franklin. Tell him what electricity is used for today.

_____

_____

_____

_____

_____

_____

STOP

0-7696-8064-X—*Science Test Practice*

Grade 4

Directions: Read the text below and study the diagram. Use information from both to help you answer questions 1–2.

Sarah and Miguel each planted a bean seed. They are using centimeter rulers to measure the bean plants that grew from the seeds.

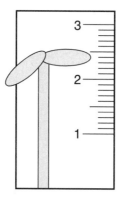 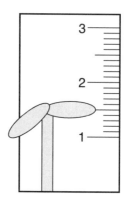

1. **How tall is Sarah's bean plant?**
    - (A) 1 cm
    - (B) 1.5 cm
    - (C) 2 cm
    - (D) 2.5 cm

2. **How tall is Miguel's bean plant?**
    - (F) 1 cm
    - (G) 1.5 cm
    - (H) 2.5 cm
    - (J) 3 cm

Directions: Read the questions. Choose the truest possible answer. Shade in the circle before your choice.

3. **Leslie needs to measure the width of the classroom. Which unit of measurement should she use?**
    - (A) meter
    - (B) kilometer
    - (C) millimeter
    - (D) centimeter

4. **Some whales migrate from the North Pole to the equator in the autumn. Which unit of measurement would be best for measuring this distance?**
    - (F) meter
    - (G) kilometer
    - (H) millimeter
    - (J) centimeter

0-7696-8064-X—*Science Test Practice*

Name_____ Date_____

Directions: Read the questions. Choose the truest possible answer. Shade in the circle before your choice.

HINT: Answer the easier questions first, and then work on the ones that are harder for you.

1. **What can a ruler be used for?**
   - Ⓐ to measure the width of a book
   - Ⓑ to measure the height of a plant
   - Ⓒ to measure the length of a key
   - Ⓓ all of the above

2. **Which are the units used when measuring with a ruler?**
   - Ⓕ inches and centimeters
   - Ⓖ inches and meters
   - Ⓗ centimeters and meters
   - Ⓙ none of the above

Directions: Study the diagram below. Use it to help you answer questions 3–6.

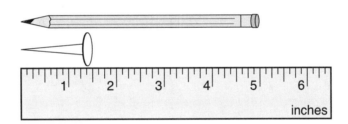

3. **How long is the nail?**
   - Ⓐ 0.5 inches
   - Ⓑ 0.5 centimeters
   - Ⓒ 1.5 inches
   - Ⓓ 1.5 centimeters

4. **How long is the pencil?**
   - Ⓕ 4.5 inches
   - Ⓖ 5 inches
   - Ⓗ 5 centimeters
   - Ⓙ 5.5 inches

5. **What is the volume of the nail?**
   - Ⓐ 0.75 inches
   - Ⓑ 1.5 inches
   - Ⓒ Nails do not have volume.
   - Ⓓ You need more information to tell.

6. **How many inches are on this ruler?**
   - Ⓕ 6 inches
   - Ⓖ 6.5 inches
   - Ⓗ 6.75 inches
   - Ⓙ 12 inches

0-7696-8064-X—*Science Test Practice*

Grade 4

Directions: Read the text below and study the table. Use information from both to help you answer questions 1–2.

This graph shows the different kinds of birds a class observed on their field trip visit. Each square represents one bird.

Birds Observed

Kinds of Birds	1	2	3	4	5	6	7	8	9	10
crows	▓	▓	▓	▓	▓	▓				
jays	▓	▓	▓	▓	▓	▓	▓			
geese	▓	▓	▓	▓	▓	▓	▓	▓	▓	▓
ducks	▓	▓	▓	▓						
chickadees	▓	▓	▓	▓	▓	▓	▓	▓	▓	▓

1. **How many of the birds seen were crows?**
   - (A) 1
   - (B) 4
   - (C) 6
   - (D) 10

2. **How many of the birds seen were geese or ducks?**
   - (F) 10
   - (G) 11
   - (H) 14
   - (J) 20

STOP

0-7696-8064-X—*Science Test Practice*

Grade 4

Directions: Study the circle graph. Use the information to help you answer questions 1–4.

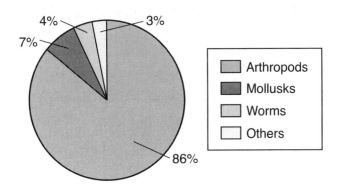

1. **According to the graph, which is the largest group of invertebrates?**

    (A) mollusks

    (B) worms

    (C) arthropods

    (D) others

2. **Other groups of invertebrates include sponges, echinoderms, and cnidarians. What percentage of all invertebrates do these animals make up?**

    (F) 3%

    (G) 4%

    (H) 7%

    (J) 86%

3. **Which type of invertebrate makes up 7% of the total?**

    (A) others

    (B) worms

    (C) mollusks

    (D) arthropods

4. **What information is NOT included in this circle graph?**

    (F) the percentage of invertebrates that are insects

    (G) the percentage of invertebrates that are mollusks

    (H) the percentage of invertebrates that are worms

    (J) the percentage of invertebrates that are arthropods

STOP

Grade 4

Directions: Read the text below. Use information from it to help you answer the questions on page 23.

HINT: Read the questions before you read the passage. Underline information in the passage that will help you answer the questions.

A Question of Mass

Marcus and Andrea were partners in science lab. Ms. Kelly gave every pair of students a balance scale. The class had to design an experiment to see if air has mass.

Ms. Kelly gave Marcus and Andrea each one balloon. "The balloons should be about the same size when you inflate them," Ms. Kelly said.

"We should blow up the balloons and see if they weigh the same," Andrea said.

"But doesn't an empty balloon have mass, too?" Marcus asked.

Andrea said, "You're right. Maybe we should put an empty balloon on each side of the scale."

Marcus put his empty balloon on the left-hand pan of the balance. Andrea put her empty balloon on the right-hand side.

"Look!" said Marcus. "They balance!"

"That must mean that the empty balloons have the same mass," said Andrea. The partners made notes in their science notebooks.

"So let's blow up both balloons!" said Andrea.

"Wait a minute," said Marcus. "How will we know how much air we're putting into the balloon? We can't be sure that when we blow into our balloons, we'll be breathing out the same amount of air."

"That's a problem," Andrea said.

They watched other lab teams blowing up both balloons and throwing them around the science lab. "Wait, I have an idea," Marcus said. He picked up one balloon and blew it up. It got bigger and bigger.

"Don't pop it, or you'll ruin our experiment!" said Andrea.

GO ON

0-7696-8064-X— Science Test Practice

Grade 4

Marcus stopped and tied the end of the balloon into a knot. "What do we know so far?" he asked Andrea with a grin.

"We know that both empty balloons had the same mass," she replied.

"And what are we trying to find out?"

Andrea stamped her foot. "You know what we're trying to do. Find out if air has mass."

They both looked at the balance.

Marcus smiled and put the inflated balloon on the balance scale.

"Wow!" Andrea said.

1. **Which hypothesis are Andrea and Marcus testing?**
   - (A) Air has no measurable mass.
   - (B) Balloons add extra mass to air.
   - (C) A balance is good for testing weight.
   - (D) Air has mass that can be measured.

2. **To test their hypothesis, which tool are Marcus and Andrea using?**
   - (F) a balance
   - (G) a spring scale
   - (H) a thermometer
   - (J) a kitchen scale

3. **In the area below, draw an image of what you think happened when Marcus put the balloon on the balance.**

STOP

========================== **Grade 4** ==========================

Directions: Read the text below and study the diagram. Use information from both to help you answer questions 1–4.

Zahra checked the temperature before going to bed. The Fahrenheit thermometer outside the window looked like picture A. When she got up in the morning, the thermometer looked like picture B.

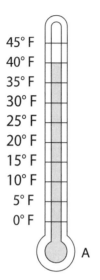
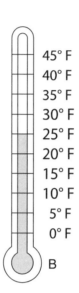

1. **What was the temperature when Zahra went to bed?**

   Ⓐ 6 degrees

   Ⓑ 30 degrees

   Ⓒ 35 degrees

   Ⓓ 40 degrees

2. **What was the temperature when Zahra got up in the morning?**

   Ⓕ 15 degrees

   Ⓖ 20 degrees

   Ⓗ 25 degrees

   Ⓙ 30 degrees

3. **How much had the temperature fallen during the night?**

   Ⓐ 5 degrees

   Ⓑ 10 degrees

   Ⓒ 15 degrees

   Ⓓ 20 degrees

4. **Which conclusion could Zahra make?**

   Ⓕ It got colder when the sun went down.

   Ⓖ The moon caused the air to get colder.

   Ⓗ The thermometer broke during the night.

   Ⓙ In the morning, the sun made the temperature rise.

0-7696-8064-X—*Science Test Practice*

Grade 4

Directions: Read the text below and study the table. Use the information to help you answer questions 1–5.

Length and distance
1 centimeter = 10 millimeters 1 meter = 100 centimeters 1 kilometer = 1,000 meters

Mass
1 kilogram = 1,000 g

Volume
1 liter = 1,000 milliliters

1. **How many millimeters are there in 14 centimeters?**
   - Ⓐ 10
   - Ⓑ 100
   - Ⓒ 110
   - Ⓓ 140

2. **Callie buys a 2-liter bottle of soda. How many milliliters has she bought?**
   - Ⓕ 150
   - Ⓖ 1,000
   - Ⓗ 1,500
   - Ⓙ 2,000

3. **Min needs to measure the depth of a large stream. Which of the following should she use?**
   - Ⓐ a centimeter ruler
   - Ⓑ a meterstick
   - Ⓒ a graduated cylinder
   - Ⓓ a beaker

4. **Which length is greatest?**
   - Ⓕ 1 m
   - Ⓖ 14 cm
   - Ⓗ 25 mm
   - Ⓙ 90 cm

5. **For his experiment, Calvin needs 100 milliliters of water. Which measuring tool should he use?**
   - Ⓐ a centimeter ruler
   - Ⓑ a meterstick
   - Ⓒ a graduated cylinder
   - Ⓓ a balance

STOP

0-7696-8064-X—*Science Test Practice*

Content Standard B

Section B of the National Science Education Standards for Grade 4 focuses on the properties of materials, the motion of objects, heat, light, magnetism, and electricity. Students will be asked to focus on material covered previously while being introduced to new aspects of that material. Section B will add to previous curriculum while allowing students to use their science skills to learn more and experience greater challenges.

Section B focuses on material objects and their place in the physical world. This includes a study of density, mass, volume, and states of matter. Material objects are also studied by examining their reaction to energy and liquids. Since this section will explore the science behind gravity, magnetism, electricity, and friction, students will be expected to demonstrate critical thinking and decision-making skills already acquired previously in this book.

Students will learn about physical objects firsthand while considering the way physical science works. Their application of science skills to this section's content is very important for achieving proper understanding of the physical environment.

Grade 4

Directions: Read the text and study the diagram below. Use it to help you answer questions 1–3.

   To be a good scientist, a student must pay very close attention to what he or she sees. When looking at an object, three very important properties to think about are the object's size, shape, and color. Compare the two objests below for size, shape, and color.

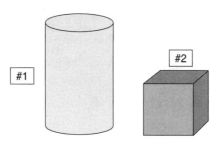

1.   **Compare their sizes:**

   _____

2.   **Compare their shapes:**

   _____

3.   **Compare their colors:**

   _____

Directions: Study the image below. Use it to help you answer question 4.

4.   **Describe the three properties of this object, being very specific about the properties. Write them below.**

   _____

   _____

   _____

STOP

   0-7696-8064-X—Science Test Practice

Name_____ Date_____

Directions: Read the questions. Choose the truest possible answer. Shade in the circle before your choice.

HINT: Come up with the answer in your head before you look at the choices. Don't let those choices trick you!

1. **Mass is the measure of the amount of matter in an object. The more matter in an object, the more mass the object has. Which of these has the greatest mass?**

   (A) a mouse
   (B) a paper clip
   (C) an elephant
   (D) a bowling ball

2. **If the strength of the earth's gravity changed, what would happen to your mass and weight?**

   (F) Your mass and weight would both change.
   (G) Your mass and weight would both stay the same.
   (H) Your mass would stay the same, and your weight would change.
   (J) Your weight would stay the same, and your mass would change.

3. **"Which weighs more, a pound of rocks or a pound of feathers?" asked Kevin.**

   "A pound of rocks, of course," said Nekia.

   "No," said Kevin. "They both weigh the same. A pound is a pound!"

   A pound of rocks and a pound of feathers may have the same weight, but they have different densities. Which one has the greatest density? How do you know?

   _____

   _____

   _____

STOP

0-7696-8064-X—*Science Test Practice*

Directions: Read the text below. Use information from it to help you answer the questions.

Matter can exist in several phases. It can be solid, liquid, or gas. The solid form of matter has the greatest density, which means its matter is pressed together very tightly. The gas form of matter is the least dense, which means that its matter is spread very far apart.

Directions: Complete questions 1–4 by writing one of the following answers from the Answer Bank in each blank. Then, shade in the circle for the correct answers for questions 5 and 6.

Answer Bank

It freezes, becoming solid ice.

It melts, becoming a liquid.

It boils, becoming a gas.

It does not change.

---

1. **What happens to a rock after sitting in the sun all day?**

   _____

2. **What happens to water when it is put in the freezer?**

   _____

3. **What happens to water in a pot on the stove, and the stove is turned on?**

   _____

4. **What happens to a cube of ice if you hold it in your hand?**

   _____

5. **Which is not a state of matter?**
   - (A) gas
   - (B) solid
   - (C) liquid
   - (D) water

6. **Keisha pours a cup of orange juice. What states of matter are the cup and the juice?**
   - (F) The cup is a gas, the juice is a liquid.
   - (G) The cup is a liquid, and the juice is a gas.
   - (H) The cup is a liquid, and the juice is a solid.
   - (J) The cup is a solid, and the juice is a liquid.

STOP

0-7696-8064-X—*Science Test Practice*

Name_____ Date_____

Directions: Read the text below. Use information from it to help you answer the questions.

Just like density and mass, volume is a characteristic of matter that can be measured. Volume tells us how much space an object takes up. The larger an object is, the more volume it has.

Directions: Rank the following items from 1 to 7 based on volume (1 is the object with the smallest volume, 7 is the object with the largest volume).

1. **penny** _____

2. **elephant** _____

3. **basketball** _____

4. **earth** _____

5. **golf ball** _____

6. **school building**

   _____

7. **chair** _____

Directions: Study the diagram below. Use it to help you answer question 8.

8. **What is the volume of the marble in the diagram to the right?**

   Ⓐ 1.5 ml
   Ⓑ 2 ml
   Ⓒ 2.5 ml
   Ⓓ 6 ml

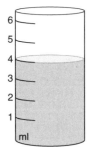
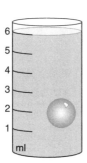

Grade 4

Directions: Read the text below. Use information from it to help you answer question 1.

You probably know that very heavy objects can float, and light objects can sink. For example, a cruise ship is many thousands of pounds in weight, but it can float. A small stone will sink, even though you can easily pick it up.

1. **What does "to float" mean?**
   - Ⓐ to hang from a rope in water
   - Ⓑ to stay on top of a liquid or gas
   - Ⓒ to drop to the bottom of a liquid or gas
   - Ⓓ to stay at the bottom of a liquid or gas

Directions: For each item, write the word "float" if you think the object will float. Write "sink" if you think the object will sink.

The following items were on the deck of a ship. When the ship ran into a storm, all the items fell into the ocean.

Example: hammer <u>sink</u>

2. rock _____

3. leaf _____

4. stapler _____

5. wood _____

6. grass _____

7. balloon _____

8. brick _____

9. feather _____

10. basketball _____

11. silver spoon _____

12. empty soda bottle _____

13. soda bottle filled with sand ____

14. rubber duck _____

15. metal clothes hanger _____

16. door key _____

STOP

0-7696-8064-X—*Science Test Practice*

Name_____   Date_____

Grade 4

Directions: Read the questions. Choose the truest possible answer. Shade in the circle before your choice.

HINT: The choice with the most information is often the correct answer.

1. **What is the name of the process in which water gets hot and turns into vapor?**

   (A) boiling

   (B) melting

   (C) freezing

   (D) dissolving

2. **When Alice starts stirring a spoonful of sugar into a glass of water, she can see the grains of sugar swirling around. After a few seconds, she cannot see the sugar anymore. What happened?**

   (F) The sugar evaporated.

   (G) The sugar dissolved and a sugar-water solution was formed.

   (H) The sugar was destroyed.

   (J) The sugar turned into water.

3. **After a thunderstorm, Michelle looked outside and saw puddles of water in a field. The next afternoon, the puddles were gone. What most likely happened?**

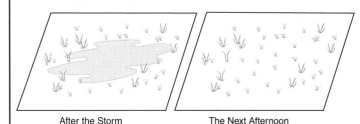

After the Storm   The Next Afternoon

   (A) The water turned into dirt.

   (B) The water froze and disappeared.

   (C) Someone came and drained the water.

   (D) The water became a gas and floated away.

4. **Kenny wants to know at what temperature water will boil. He puts a Centigrade thermometer in a pan of boiling water. What will the thermometer read?**

   (F) 0° Fahrenheit

   (G) 100° Fahrenheit

   (H) 0° Celsius

   (J) 100° Celsius

STOP

0-7696-8064-X—*Science Test Practice*

Name_____ Date_____

Directions: Read the text below. Use information from it to help you answer the questions.

Matter can exist by itself, but it can also be combined with other substances. A mixture is the combination of different types of matter. In a mixture, none of the matter combines chemically. For example, a salad is a mixture of lettuce, tomatoes, cucumbers, or other types of vegetables.

Each part of the salad is exactly the same matter that it was before being added to the salad. The lettuce is still lettuce, and the tomatoes are still tomatoes. The only difference is that now they are mixed together with other vegetables. Mixtures can involve solids, liquids, and gases.

Directions: Write an example of each of the following types of mixtures on the line.

Example: A solid and a gas <u>dust particles floating in the air</u>

1. **A solid and a solid** _____

2. **A gas and a gas** _____

3. **A gas and a liquid** _____

4. **A liquid and a liquid** _____

Directions: Read the text below. Use information from it to help you answer question 5.

A special type of mixture is called a solution. A solution is a mixture where all the parts are completely combined. All of the parts of a solution are evenly spread throughout the solution.

5. **A glass of water is pictured to the right. Imagine that you just mixed a spoonful of salt into this water, and the salt dissolved. Place 10 X's throughout the water to show how the salt could be spread through the water. (Example: If you think the salt should stay at the bottom of the water after being dissolved, you can put all 10 X's along the bottom of the glass.)**

Name_____ Date_____

Directions: Read the question. Choose the truest possible answer. Shade in the circle before your choice.

1. **The Law of Conservation of Energy states that _____ .**

    Ⓐ   energy cannot be created or destroyed

    Ⓑ   we cannot use more energy than we need

    Ⓒ   greater amounts of matter hold more energy

    Ⓓ   energy must always be part of the atmosphere

Directions: Use the words in the Word Bank to fill in the blanks.

Word Bank

light   sound   kinetic   potential   electrical   gravitational

---

The ball started at the top of the stairs, full of **2.** _____ energy. When Jonathan pushed it, the energy became **3.** _____ as the ball moved quickly down the stairs.

"Could you please make a little less noise?" Jonathan's mother asked. The **4.** _____ energy bothered her.

"And please don't let the ball break the lamp." They needed the lamp for **5.** _____ energy so they could see. All the **6.** _____ energy in the world would not help if the bulb was broken.

Name_____ Date_____

Directions: Read the questions. Choose the truest possible answer. Shade in the circle before your choice.

1. **When light passes through a glass of water, the light bends. This is called _____ .**

   (A) reflection
   (B) refraction
   (C) absorption
   (D) obstruction

2. **A green leaf _____ green light.**

   (F) reflects
   (G) refracts
   (H) absorbs
   (J) obstructs

3. **If you shine white light on a prism, what will you see on the other side?**

   (A) white light
   (B) many colors
   (C) your shadow
   (D) your reflection

4. **How does light usually travel?**

   (F) in all directions
   (G) in a straight line
   (H) toward dark points
   (J) toward human eyes

5. **Roberto looks into a concave mirror. He sees himself as being _____ than he really is.**

   (A) taller
   (B) closer
   (C) farther
   (D) shorter

Directions: Read the question. Write your answer on the lines provided.

6. **Why does a prism have the effect you chose in question 3?**

   _____

   _____

   _____

   _____

0-7696-8064-X—*Science Test Practice*

Name_____ Date_____

Directions: Read the questions. Choose the truest possible answer. Shade in the circle before your choice.

1. **What causes the eardrum to vibrate?**
   - Ⓐ Tiny bones move.
   - Ⓑ The ear feels pain.
   - Ⓒ Sound waves hit it.
   - Ⓓ Silence surrounds it.

2. **What is the effect of the inner ear's vibration?**
   - Ⓕ The inner ear's walls are lined with hairs.
   - Ⓖ Vibrations pass through middle ear bones.
   - Ⓗ Nerve cells send sound signals to the brain.
   - Ⓙ The outer ear collects and guides sound waves.

3. **When you yell, your vocal chords _____ .**
   - Ⓐ stay open widely
   - Ⓑ take in a lot of air
   - Ⓒ become long and thin
   - Ⓓ move back and forth

Directions: Read each question. Write your answers on the lines provided.

4. **Why does sound move more quickly through solids than through gases?**

   _____

   _____

5. **Name one behavior of light that is similar to the behavior of sound in an echo? Explain your answer.**

   _____

   _____

6. **In what form does sound travel through matter?**

   _____

   _____

0-7696-8064-X—*Science Test Practice*

Grade 4

Directions: Read the questions. Choose the truest possible answer. Shade in the circle before your choice.

1. **Thermal energy is another name for _____ .**

   - Ⓐ heat
   - Ⓑ energy
   - Ⓒ movement
   - Ⓓ magnetism

2. **How do you know there is thermal energy?**

   - Ⓕ You can feel heat.
   - Ⓖ You can see an object move.
   - Ⓗ You can see something move.
   - Ⓙ You can hear something make noise.

3. **If you add thermal energy to matter, what happens?**

   - Ⓐ The particles disappear.
   - Ⓑ The particles stop moving.
   - Ⓒ The particles move faster.
   - Ⓓ The particles move more slowly.

Directions: Read each question. Write your answers on the lines provided.

4. **If all the particles in a metal spoon start moving faster, how has the spoon's temperature changed?**

   _____

   _____

5. **Give two examples of thermal energy.**

   _____

   _____

0-7696-8064-X—*Science Test Practice*

Grade 4

Directions: Read the questions. Choose the truest possible answer. Shade in the circle before your choice.

HINT: Don't be too quick to change your answers. Your first answer may be correct, unless you read the question incorrectly the first time.

1. **Charge is the measure of extra positive or _____ particles.**
   - (A) still
   - (B) light
   - (C) white
   - (D) negative

2. **What is the relationship between an electric force and an electric field?**
   - (F) They are opposites.
   - (G) They are the same thing.
   - (H) Electric field occurs within an electric force.
   - (J) The electric field is where electric forces occur.

3. **Static charge can become moving charge. What is this moving charge called?**
   - (A) parallel circuit
   - (B) mover charge
   - (C) current events
   - (D) electrical current

4. **What is an electrical circuit?**
   - (F) a path for electric current
   - (G) a path for a battery
   - (H) a path for wires to follow
   - (J) a circular movement

5. **Which of the following is *least* likely to use electricity?**
   - (A) refrigerator
   - (B) bathtub
   - (C) television
   - (D) computer

Directions: Read each question. Write your answers on the lines provided.

6. **Give two examples of items that use electricity that you use in your everyday life.**

   _____

   _____

7. **Give an example of when you have experienced static electricity.**

   _____

   _____

STOP

0-7696-8064-X—*Science Test Practice*

Directions: Read the questions. Choose the truest possible answer. Shade in the circle before your choice.

1. **Copper is a "conductor." What does this tell you about copper?**
   - (A) It can bend easily.
   - (B) It is always very cold.
   - (C) Light reflects off of it brightly.
   - (D) Electrical current can pass through it easily.

2. **Rory's father was working on the electrical wiring in his basement. Rory noticed that his father wore rubber gloves when he touched the wires. Rory's father told him it was because the rubber gloves did not conduct electricity. The gloves protected him from the current in the wires. Which of the following would you call the gloves?**
   - (F) a battery
   - (G) a resistor
   - (H) an insulator
   - (J) a conductor

3. **Parallel circuits are different from series circuits because they have more _____ .**
   - (A) bulbs
   - (B) paths
   - (C) power
   - (D) batteries

Directions: Read each question. Write your answer on the lines provided.

4. **What does a battery do?**

   _____

   _____

   _____

Directions: Study the diagram below. Use it to help you answer question 5.

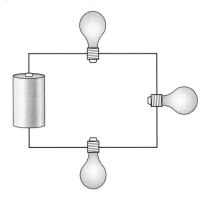

5. **When the switch on a circuit is closed, the light turns on. Explain why this happens.**

   _____

   _____

   _____

STOP

0-7696-8064-X—*Science Test Practice*

Grade 4

Directions: Read the text below. Use information from it to help you answer the questions on the next page.

Mark and his parents were at his grandma's house. Mark was not very interested in the adults' conversation.

Grandma noticed him fidgeting. "Hold on a second, Mark. I have something that might keep you occupied." She went into the basement, and came back with a small box full of black bars of different sizes.

"What are they?" asked Mark.

"They're magnets," Grandma explained. "See what you can do with them."

Mark opened the box and pulled out the longest, widest magnet. Well, he only tried to pull that bar out. A smaller magnet stuck to the end of it. He shook the bigger magnet to make the small one fall off. It didn't.

He tried holding the big magnet upside down. The small magnet would have to fall if it had nothing under it, right? The magnets stayed attached. Finally, Mark pulled the magnets apart with his hands. They came apart, but it was harder than Mark had expected. It felt like the magnets wanted to stay together.

Mark took a medium-sized magnet out of the box. Would the big magnet be able to hold this one? He tried to pick it up by one end. This time, the result was different. It felt like one magnet was pushing the other away. When he tried to push the magnets together with both hands, it felt like something was in between them, pushing them apart. Finally, he turned the medium magnet around. Now, the big one picked it up easily.

Mark thanked his grandma for giving him something to do. Now, all he wanted was someone to explain why the magnets worked this way.

0-7696-8064-X—*Science Test Practice*

HINT: Look at question 1. The answer choices have a lot of information. If even one word of a choice is wrong, that choice is not the answer.

1. **Which may be the reason the big magnet picked up the small magnet?**

   (A) The S pole of the big magnet faced the S pole of the small magnet.

   (B) The N pole of the big magnet faced the S pole of the small magnet.

   (C) Either pole of the big magnet faced either pole of the small magnet.

   (D) The N pole of the big magnet faced the N pole of the small magnet.

2. **Why did Mark feel like the big magnet and the medium-sized magnet were pushing each other away?**

   _____

   _____

   _____

   _____

   _____

   _____

3. **What changed when Mark turned the medium magnet around?**

   _____

   _____

   _____

4. **How would you explain the way a compass works to Mark?**

   _____

   _____

   _____

   _____

   _____

   _____

   _____

STOP

0-7696-8064-X—*Science Test Practice*

Grade 4

Directions: Read the questions. Choose the truest possible answer. Shade in the circle before your choice.

1. Lenora is on a train. She knows that the train is in motion. So she knows that the train is _____ .
   - (A) changing its fuel
   - (B) changing direction
   - (C) changing position
   - (D) changing altitude

2. Velocity describes speed and _____ .
   - (F) time
   - (G) distance
   - (H) direction
   - (J) momentum

Directions: Read each question. Write your answers on the lines provided.

3. What is inertia?

_____

_____

_____

_____

4. The harder you hit a tennis ball, the farther it will travel. Give one reason why this is true.

_____

_____

_____

5. A car is moving down the highway. One person says the car is traveling at 50km/hour. Another person says the car is moving at 1500 km/hour. A third person says the car is moving at 5000 km/hour. This is an example of relative motion. Explain how all three people can be correct.

_____

_____

_____

_____

STOP

Grade 4

Directions: Read the question. Choose the truest possible answer. Shade in the circle before your choice.

1. **It is easiest to slide while wearing socks on a _____ floor.**
    - (A) tiled
    - (B) wood
    - (D) carpeted
    - (C) rubber

Directions: Read the question. Write your answer on the lines provided.

2. **What two factors determine the strength of gravity between two objects?**

    _____

    _____

    _____

Directions: Study the diagram below. Use it to help you answer question 3.

Sun

Earth

Mars

 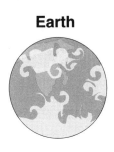 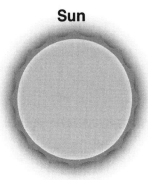

3. **What are two reasons that the pull of gravity between Mars and the Sun is less than the pull of gravity between the earth and the sun?**

    _____

    _____

    _____

    _____

STOP

━━━ _Grade 4_ ━━━

Directions: Study the diagrams below. Use them to help you answer the questions.

HINT: Relax. If you feel too nervous to work, stop for a minute.

1. **What kind of simple machine is being used to move the bucket?**

   _____

2. **How does this kind of simple machine change the way the work is done?**

   _____

   _____

3. **What kind of simple machine is used to raise the student?**

   _____

   _____

   _____

4. **Give another example of how you might use this kind of simple machine.**

   _____

   _____

   _____

STOP

Content Standard C

Section C of the National Science Education Standards emphasizes the study of the living earth. Students will be encouraged to go beyond basic scientific similarities and differences of living things. Emphasis is placed on critical thinking about how various aspects of living things affect the earth.

While examining the basic needs and structures of living things, students will be asked to formulate questions that demonstrate critical thinking skills. Students will examine ecosystems, life cycles, and food webs to determine how animals affect their environments.

Students will pursue a rigorous overview of organisms and their life functions, from the most basic level to more advanced study.

0-7696-8064-X—*Science Test Practice*

Grade 4

Directions: Read the questions. Choose the truest possible answer. Shade in the circle before your choice.

1. **What is the classification of living things called?**
   - Ⓐ biology
   - Ⓑ astrology
   - Ⓒ taxonomy
   - Ⓓ astronomy

2. **Who created the system that scientists use to classify living things?**
   - Ⓕ Albert Einstein
   - Ⓖ Charles Darwin
   - Ⓗ Thomas Edison
   - Ⓙ Carolus Linnaeus

3. **Animals and plants are classified using a 7-part system. The first part of the system is called a kingdom. How many kingdoms are there?**
   - Ⓐ 2
   - Ⓑ 3
   - Ⓒ 4
   - Ⓓ 5

4. **Animals and plants are both _____ .**
   - Ⓕ classes
   - Ⓖ species
   - Ⓗ kingdoms
   - Ⓙ monerans

5. **The classification system is similar to a _____ .**
   - Ⓐ family tree
   - Ⓑ class roster
   - Ⓒ flight of stairs
   - Ⓓ book glossary

6. **To which kingdom do mammals belong?**
   - Ⓕ fungi
   - Ⓖ plants
   - Ⓙ protists
   - Ⓗ animals

STOP

0-7696-8064-X—*Science Test Practice*

Grade 4

Directions: Read the questions. Choose the truest possible answer. Shade in the circle before your choice.

1. Which living thing is NOT an animal?

- (A) bird
- (B) flower
- (C) spider monkey
- (D) groundhog

2. What are all plants and animals made of?

- (F) fur
- (G) cells
- (H) circuits
- (J) instinctive matter

3. Where do animals live?

- (A) in trees
- (B) underwater
- (C) underground
- (D) all of the above

4. What is it called when one animal watches another animal in order to learn something?

- (F) impulse
- (G) instinct
- (H) observation
- (J) communication

Directions: Read the question. Write your answer on the lines provided.

5. Why do scientists classify animals?

_____

_____

_____

_____

_____

STOP

0-7696-8064-X—Science Test Practice

Grade 4

Directions: Study the diagram. Use it to help you answer questions 1–3.

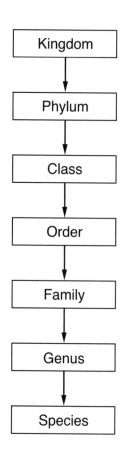

1. Animals with backbones are all in the same _____ .

   Ⓐ order
   Ⓑ class
   Ⓒ phylum
   Ⓓ family

2. Which of the following groups includes animals that are NOT vertebrates?

   Ⓕ reptiles
   Ⓖ mollusks
   Ⓗ mammals
   Ⓙ amphibians

3. To which group do birds and fish belong?

   Ⓐ reptiles
   Ⓑ mammals
   Ⓒ vertebrates
   Ⓓ amphibians

Directions: Read the question. Write your answer on the lines provided.

4. List two characteristics that all birds have. Then, list two ways that birds can be different from each other.

_____

_____

_____

_____

_____

0-7696-8064-X—*Science Test Practice*

Grade 4

Directions: Read the questions. Choose the truest possible answer. Shade in the circle before your choice.

1. **Which animal is an invertebrate?**
   - (A) dog
   - (B) snail
   - (C) panda
   - (D) monkey

2. **Which animals are part of the arthropod group?**
   - (F) snakes and worms
   - (G) snails, snakes, and turtles
   - (H) vertebrates and invertebrates
   - (J) insects, spiders, and scorpions

3. **Which of the following is a mollusk?**
   - (A) cat
   - (B) bird
   - (C) toad
   - (D) clam

4. **What do mollusks have in common with arthropods?**
   - (F) They live in shells.
   - (G) They do not have legs.
   - (H) They are invertebrates.
   - (J) They all live underground.

Directions: Study the diagram below. Use it to help you answer questions 5–6.

5. **Though invertebrates do not have an internal skeleton, they do have features that are beneficial. Referring to the picture above, name two characteristics that may help this invertebrate survive.**

   _____

   _____

6. **Name three different invertebrates and describe their similarities.**

   _____

   _____

   _____

0-7696-8064-X—*Science Test Practice*

Grade 4

Directions: Read the questions. Choose the truest possible answer. Shade in the circle before your choice.

1. **What is the right climate for animals?**
   - (A) cold with lots of clouds and rain
   - (B) hot with no rain and lots of sun
   - (C) different temperatures for different animals
   - (D) mid-range temperatures with partly sunny skies

2. **Animals can survive only in habitats where _____ .**
   - (F) the sun shines brightly
   - (G) there is not enough food
   - (H) their basic needs can be met
   - (J) there are both vertebrates and invertebrates

3. **How does a goat get energy from grass?**
   - (A) by digesting it and fueling the body
   - (B) by looking at it
   - (C) by breathing it in
   - (D) by sleeping on it

Directions: Read each question. Write your answers on the lines provided.

4. **Living things need to be in the right environment to survive. Choose one living thing and name four characteristics that its environment provides.**

   _____

   _____

   _____

5. **Why do animals need air?**

   _____

   _____

   _____

STOP

0-7696-8064-X—Science Test Practice

Grade 4

Directions: Read the questions. Choose the truest possible answer. Shade in the circle before your choice.

HINT: Offspring is another way of saying children.

1. **Animals need to reproduce so that _____ .**
    - (A) they will find food
    - (B) they will stay healthy
    - (C) predators will not attack them
    - (D) their species will not disappear

2. **Butterflies have four stages of life: egg, larva, pupa, and adult. This change is called _____ .**
    - (F) hypnosis
    - (G) migration
    - (H) hibernation
    - (J) metamorphosis

3. **How many offspring do most mammals have?**
    - (A) one
    - (B) a few
    - (C) hundreds
    - (D) at least twelve

4. **When an insect lays eggs, how many does it usually lay?**
    - (F) two
    - (G) twenty
    - (H) twenty-two
    - (J) hundreds

Directions: Read each question. Write your answers on the lines provided.

5. **When do most mammals leave their mothers?**

    _____

    _____

    _____

    _____

6. **List four different types of animals that lay eggs.**

    _____

    _____

    _____

STOP

0-7696-8064-X—*Science Test Practice*

Grade 4

Directions: Read the questions. Choose the truest possible answer. Shade in the circle before your choice.

1. **What are the two main groups of plants?**
   - Ⓐ biotic and abiotic
   - Ⓑ vascular and nonvascular
   - Ⓒ producers and consumers
   - Ⓓ vertebrates and invertebrates

2. **Which of the following is NOT a plant?**
   - Ⓕ grass
   - Ⓖ weeds
   - Ⓗ shrimp
   - Ⓙ flowers

3. **Sunflowers and pine trees *both* have _____ .**
   - Ⓐ cones
   - Ⓑ seeds
   - Ⓒ petals
   - Ⓓ needles

4. **Mosses reproduce using _____ .**
   - Ⓕ roots
   - Ⓖ seeds
   - Ⓗ leaves
   - Ⓙ spores

5. **What does vascular mean?**
   - Ⓐ with tubes
   - Ⓑ like a collar
   - Ⓒ like vampires
   - Ⓓ square shaped

6. **Which of the following is a nonvascular plant?**
   - Ⓕ a fern
   - Ⓖ tree moss
   - Ⓗ an oak tree
   - Ⓙ a chestnut tree

Directions: Read the question. Write your answer on the lines provided.

7. **Why do most mosses live on rocks?**

   _____

   _____

   _____

   _____

   _____

STOP

Grade 4

Directions: Read the questions. Choose the truest possible answer. Shade in the circle before your choice.

1. **What do all plants need?**
   - Ⓐ air, nutrients, dirt, and light
   - Ⓑ oxygen, dirt, water, and light
   - Ⓒ air, nutrients, water, and light
   - Ⓓ oxygen, nutrients, water, and light

2. **Most plants get their nutrients directly from _____ .**
   - Ⓕ the air
   - Ⓖ the soil
   - Ⓗ animals
   - Ⓙ other plants

3. **What do plants give off during photosynthesis?**
   - Ⓐ water
   - Ⓑ oxygen
   - Ⓒ sunlight
   - Ⓓ carbon dioxide

4. **A plant produces _____ through photosynthesis and then uses it for energy.**
   - Ⓕ sugar
   - Ⓖ water
   - Ⓗ oxygen
   - Ⓙ carbon dioxide

Directions: Read the question. Write your answer on the lines provided.

5. **Both plants and animals need air to survive. What part of the air do plants use? What part of the air do animals use?**

_____

_____

_____

_____

STOP

0-7696-8064-X—*Science Test Practice*

Name_____   Date_____

Grade 4

Directions: Read the text below. Use information from it to help you answer questions 1–4.

When living things make more living things like them, it is called reproduction. Flowering plants reproduce by pollination. Most animals reproduce with sperm and eggs.

1. **Name three ways seeds can spread.**

    _____

    _____

2. **Under the right conditions, seeds will germinate. To germinate is to** _____ .

    Ⓐ spread
    Ⓑ sprout
    Ⓒ reproduce
    Ⓓ photosynthesize

3. **What three things do seeds need in order to germinate?**

    _____

    _____

    _____

4. **Bees have pockets in their legs. These pockets fill with seeds when a bee lands on the flower of a plant. As the bee flies away, the seeds in the pockets spill out onto the ground. How has the bee helped the plant?**

    _____

    _____

    _____

Directions: Using the words in the Word Bank, label the reproductive parts of the plant below.

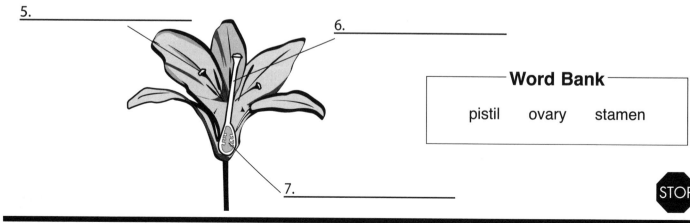

5. _____

6. _____

7. _____

┌─ **Word Bank** ─┐
pistil   ovary   stamen

STOP

0-7696-8064-X—*Science Test Practice*

Name_____ Date_____

Directions: Study the diagram below. Use it to help you answer questions 1–4.

Life Cycle of a Frog

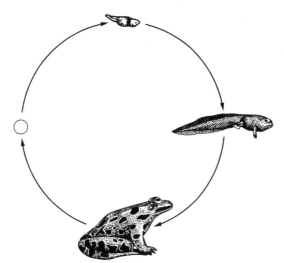

1. Seeds are to plants as _____ are to frogs.
    - (A) tails
    - (B) eggs
    - (C) parents
    - (D) tadpoles

2. An organism is considered to be an adult when it can _____ .
    - (F) reproduce
    - (G) obtain food
    - (H) protect itself
    - (J) reach up high

3. List two similarities between the life cycle of a plant and the life cycle of an animal.

    _____

    _____

4. Choose an animal besides the frog. In the space below, create a diagram of its life cycle. Include 3 steps in the life cycle.

STOP

   0-7696-8064-X—*Science Test Practice*

Grade 4

Directions: Read the questions. Choose the truest possible answer. Shade in the circle before your choice.

1. In a swamp, many organisms live together. A swamp is an example of a(n) _____ .
   - (A) biosystem
   - (B) ecosystem
   - (C) plant system
   - (D) animal system

2. In order for living things to live in an ecosystem, the ecosystem must contain their _____ .
   - (F) parents
   - (G) offspring
   - (H) basic needs
   - (J) main predator

3. Deer live in many different areas in a certain park. Deer are one of the many _____ in the park.
   - (A) families
   - (B) kingdoms
   - (C) populations
   - (D) communities

4. Honeybees get nectar from flowers and use it as food. They also help flowers reproduce. Therefore, honeybees and flowers are part of the same _____ .
   - (F) family
   - (G) phylum
   - (H) population
   - (J) community

Directions: Read each question. Write your answers on the lines provided.

5. How does energy get into the soil?

   _____

   _____

6. Name two living and three nonliving parts of an ecosystem.

   _____

   _____

7. Give two reasons why it can be dangerous to bring new organisms into an ecosystem.

   _____

   _____

   _____

STOP

0-7696-8064-X—Science Test Practice

Name_____ Date_____

Directions: Read the questions. Choose the truest possible answer. Shade in the circle before your choice.

1. Hunting mice can be described as the _____ of owls.
   - (A) niche
   - (B) habitat
   - (C) population
   - (D) ecosystem

2. Which two animals can live in the same habitat?
   - (F) a jellyfish and a dog
   - (G) a toucan and a swan
   - (H) a snake and a monkey
   - (J) a penguin and a camel

3. In which ecosystem is the population density of sparrows the highest?
   - (A) a large area with few sparrows
   - (B) a large area with many sparrows
   - (C) a small area with few sparrows
   - (D) a small area with many sparrows

Directions: Read each question. Write your answers on the lines provided.

4. What is a habitat?

   _____

   _____

5. What are two characteristics of the place where you live that make it a good habitat for you?

   _____

   _____

6. Imagine a species that eats plants, prefers cold temperatures, and likes to live underground. Describe a good habitat for this species.

   _____

   _____

   _____

STOP

0-7696-8064-X—*Science Test Practice*

Name_____   Date_____

Grade 4

Directions: Read the questions. Choose the truest possible answer. Shade in the circle before your choice.

1. **What does a carnivore eat?**
   - (A) dirt
   - (B) rocks
   - (C) plants
   - (D) animals

2. **What is an animal that only eats plants?**
   - (F) a carnivore
   - (G) a herbivore
   - (H) an omnivore
   - (J) a plantivore

3. **What does an omnivore eat?**
   - (A) only plants
   - (B) only meat
   - (C) sunlight and air
   - (D) plants and animals

4. **What do herbivores and omnivores have in common?**
   - (F) They both eat meat.
   - (G) They both eat plants.
   - (H) Neither of them eats meat.
   - (J) Neither of them eats vegetables.

Directions: Read the text below. Use information from it to help you answer questions 5–6.

In the grasslands, prairie grasses make their own food. Grasshoppers eat the prairie grasses. Snakes eat the grasshoppers, and then hawks eat the snakes.

5. **In the passage, snakes are _____.**
   - (A) omnivores
   - (B) carnivores
   - (C) herbivores
   - (D) producers

6. **Draw a food chain below showing the situation described in the passage.**

0-7696-8064-X—Science Test Practice

Grade 4

Directions: Read the questions. Choose the truest possible answer. Shade in the circle before your choice.

1. **Over time, grassland might turn into a forest. This change is called _____.**

    (A) nutrition
    (B) recession
    (C) extinction
    (D) succession

2. **A fire burns down all the trees in a forest. What is likely to happen in about a year?**

    (F) All the trees will come back.
    (G) Only dead trees will be there.
    (H) Mosses and lichens will grow.
    (J) New kinds of animals will come.

Directions: Read each question. Write your answers on the lines provided.

3. **When organisms die, how do they help new organisms to grow?**

    _____

    _____

    _____

4. **Why do you think populations that are spread through several areas are *less* likely to become extinct than populations that are all in one area?**

    _____

    _____

    _____

    _____

5. **Name one thing humans can do to help keep endangered animals from becoming extinct.**

    _____

    _____

0-7696-8064-X—*Science Test Practice*

Name_____ Date_____

Grade 4

Directions: Read the questions. Choose the truest possible answer. Shade in the circle before your choice.

1. **How does the destruction of the rainforest affect coral reefs?**
   - Ⓐ It causes it to rain more, which floods the coral reefs.
   - Ⓑ Forest soil washes out to coral reefs and kills the animals.
   - Ⓒ People use coral reef resources after the rainforests have died.
   - Ⓓ The animals from the rainforests must go to live in the coral reefs.

2. **What can people do to stop harming ecosystems?**
   - Ⓕ drive cars often
   - Ⓖ drink enough milk
   - Ⓗ use recycled paper
   - Ⓙ ride bikes with a helmet

3. **Kit uses old newspapers to cover the floor when she paints. This is an example of _____ .**
   - Ⓐ recycling
   - Ⓑ stabilizing
   - Ⓒ reclamation
   - Ⓓ conservation

4. **Avi is careful to turn off the water when he is not using it. This is an example of _____ .**
   - Ⓕ recycling
   - Ⓖ stabilizing
   - Ⓗ reclamation
   - Ⓙ conservation

5. **A group of people try to clean up a lake after an oil spill. This is an example of _____ .**
   - Ⓐ recycling
   - Ⓑ stabilizing
   - Ⓒ reclamation
   - Ⓓ conservation

Directions: Read the question. Write your answer on the lines provided.

6. **How might people harm the rainforest?**

_____

_____

_____

0-7696-8064-X—*Science Test Practice*

Grade 4

Directions: Read the questions. Choose the truest possible answer. Shade in the circle before your choice.

1. **A plant on the windowsill seems to bend toward the sun. This shows that the plant can _____ .**
   - (A) undergo germination
   - (B) break down its cell walls
   - (C) grow taller than its parent
   - (D) respond to its environment

2. **Monarch butterflies migrate south for the winter. This is an example of _____ .**
   - (F) instinct
   - (G) hunting
   - (H) mimicry
   - (J) gathering

Directions: Read each question. Write your answers on the lines provided

3. **Write a definition for the word *instinct*.**

   _____

   _____

   _____

4. **A mouse in an open field sees a shadow and hears a hawk cry. Explain what the mouse may do to protect itself.**

   _____

   _____

5. **Give examples of an action or actions you take in response to your environment. What factors make you do this?**

   _____

   _____

   _____

   _____

   _____

   _____

STOP

 0-7696-8064-X—*Science Test Practice*

Grade 4

Directions: Read the questions. Choose the truest possible answer. Shade in the circle before your choice.

HINT: Stimuli are anything that causes a reaction. Stimuli is the plural form and means more than one stimulus.

1. **To detect stimuli, living things have special cells called _____ .**
   - (A) animal cells
   - (B) bodily organs
   - (C) mammary glands
   - (D) sensory receptors

2. **"When Mom cooks apple pie, it makes the whole house smell so good! I salivate when I smell it." What is the stimulus?**
   - (F) an apple pie
   - (G) salivary glands working
   - (H) the smell of the apple pie
   - (J) the smell of the house

3. **Which of the following is an example of reacting to a stimulus?**
   - (A) A painting falls off the wall.
   - (B) It rains and a puddle forms.
   - (C) A shirt is too small so you stretch it out.
   - (D) You pull your hand back from a hot surface.

4. **When you get goose bumps, they might be from surrounding stimuli such as _____ .**
   - (F) cold air
   - (G) warm water
   - (H) colored walls
   - (J) none of the above

Directions: Read each question. Write your answers on the lines provided.

5. **List two examples of times when you have reacted to stimuli.**

_____

_____

_____

6. **Wallace accidentally touches a hot stove. Immediately, his hand starts to hurt. What advantage might there be to feeling this kind of pain?**

_____

_____

_____

STOP

Grade 4

Directions: Read the questions. Choose the truest possible answer. Shade in the circle before your choice.

1. **How does a producer get its food?**
   - (A) It does not need food.
   - (B) It makes its own food.
   - (C) It eats other living things.
   - (D) It eats food made by other living things.

2. **A food chain describes the way _____ moves through ecosystems.**
   - (F) water
   - (G) plants
   - (H) energy
   - (J) animals

3. **What is the name for a living thing that cannot make its own food?**
   - (A) a plant
   - (B) a producer
   - (C) an organism
   - (D) a consumer

4. **A consumer can get energy by _____ .**
   - (F) eating a producer
   - (G) eating a decomposer
   - (H) decomposing another consumer
   - (J) combining sunlight, water, and carbon dioxide

Directions: Study the diagram to the right. Use it to help you answer questions 5–6.

5. **What relationship do rabbits have with snakes?**
   - (A) Snakes eat rabbits.
   - (B) Rabbits eat snakes.
   - (C) Rabbits and snakes both eat grass.
   - (D) Eagles are eaten by snakes.

6. **People are moving into the area where these animals live. They are putting out poison to kill the snakes in the area. How will that affect the rabbit population?**

_____

_____

_____

0-7696-8064-X—*Science Test Practice*

Grade 4

Directions: Study the diagram below. Use it to help you answer questions 1–3.

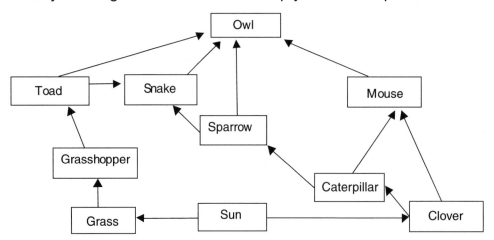

1. **A food web is _____ .**
   - (A) a pack of animals
   - (B) a group of ecosystems
   - (C) a list of related food types
   - (D) a set of linked food chains

2. **What is the main source of energy for all things in a food web?**
   - (F) soil
   - (G) water
   - (H) grass
   - (J) the sun

3. **In the space below, draw two possible food chains from the food web that include insects. On the lines, explain how the energy travels in each food chain.**

_____

_____

_____

_____

0-7696-8064-X— *Science Test Practice*

Name_____ Date_____

Grade 4

Directions: Read the questions. Choose the truest possible answer. Shade in the circle before your choice.

1. A(n) _____ is a body part or behavior that helps an animal meet its needs in its environment.
   - (A) conservation
   - (B) adaptation
   - (C) observation
   - (D) sensation

2. A tiger's fur is striped to help it blend in with the light and shadows of the tall grass. This is an example of _____ .
   - (F) mimicry
   - (G) instinct
   - (H) migration
   - (J) camouflage

3. An insect called a walking stick looks very much like a twig. This is an example of _____ .
   - (A) mimicry
   - (B) instinct
   - (C) migration
   - (D) camouflage

4. Tigers know how to hunt because they _____ .
   - (F) are born knowing
   - (G) learn from baby tigers
   - (H) learn from adult tigers
   - (J) figure it out themselves

Directions: Read the questions. Write your answers on the lines provided.

5. Polar bears live in the Arctic. They have white fur. How might their white fur help polar bears survive?

_____

_____

6. Toucans eat fruits that grow high in trees. What feature of the toucan's body structure might be an adaptation? Explain your answer.

_____

_____

_____

_____

_____

STOP

0-7696-8064-X—*Science Test Practice*

Grade 4

Directions: Read the question. Choose the truest possible answer. Shade in the circle before your choice.

1. **A(n) _____ is the mark or remains of a living thing that died thousands or millions of years ago.**

     (A) mold
     (B) fossil
     (C) emboss
     (D) extinction

Directions: Read each question. Write your answers on the lines provided.

2. **How can scientists learn about species that have been extinct for a long time?**

     _____

     _____

     _____

3. **A scientist wants to find out what type of food a certain animal ate. Which fossil might she study from that animal?**

     _____

     _____

Directions: Study the diagram below. Use it to help you answer question 4.

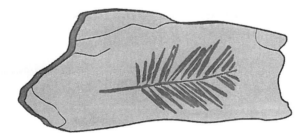

4. **What is one thing you can infer from this fossil?**

     _____

STOP

Content Standard D

Section D takes a critical approach to the understanding of the earth, its materials, and its relationship to the rest of the cosmos. From the vantage point of the earth, students will examine the solar system, its planets, asteroids, comets, and size. In this context, students will take a new look at the earth's atmosphere, layers, and cycles.

Students will learn about the earth and apply the scientific methods from previous sections to gain certain knowledge about our planet and its various cycles. Included are erosion, precipitation, deposition, and natural disasters like landslides, earthquakes, volcanoes, and weather phenomena.

Section D acquaints students with most of the basic processes that keep the earth stable and make it a special planet in our solar system and in the universe.

0-7696-8064-X—*Science Test Practice*

Grade 4

Directions: Read the text below. Use information from it to help you answer the questions.

Close to a hundred years ago, a scientist named Alfred Wegener came up with an idea. He was studying animal fossils. Many of the fossils from different parts of the world looked like they came from similar animals.

Wegener looked at a map of the world. He noticed that the continents looked like they could fit together, just like puzzle pieces.

Could it be that all of these different pieces of land used to be one big continent? That would explain why similar animals lived on the different continents.

Wegener thought that he was right, but he could not prove it. He strongly believed that the continents started off as one big piece of land, which he called Pangaea. According to his theory, those continents then drifted apart.

Other scientists teased Wegener for his ideas. They told him that he could not explain how the continents moved like that.

Oceanographers and geologists in the 1950's and 1960's were able to confirm evidence of continental drifting, thus supporting Wegener's theory.

1. **What term would best describe Wegener's theory?**

   Ⓐ fossil drift
   Ⓑ continental drift
   Ⓒ animal exploration
   Ⓓ oceanic exploration

2. **How did Wegener's theory help to explain his discovery about animal fossils?**

   _____

   _____

   _____

   _____

   _____

   _____

   _____

0-7696-8064-X—*Science Test Practice*

Grade 4

Directions: Fill in the first column of the chart below with the names of rocks from the Word Bank.

┌─────────── **Word Bank** ───────────┐

sedimentary   metamorphic
igneous

└─────────────────────────────────────┘

Type of Rock	Forms When...
1._____	molten rock hardens
2._____	sediment hardens and "glues" together
3._____	rocks are changed by heat or pressure

Directions: Read the questions. Choose the truest possible answer. Shade in the circle before your choice.

4. **What type of rock might be formed from the contents of an erupted volcano?**
   - Ⓐ igneous
   - Ⓑ crystalline
   - Ⓒ sedimentary
   - Ⓓ metamorphic

5. **When the water in salt lakes and seas evaporates, it leaves the salt behind. The salt dries, forming a type of rock called halite. What type of rock is halite?**
   - Ⓕ igneous
   - Ⓖ crystalline
   - Ⓗ sedimentary
   - Ⓙ metamorphic

6. **Steve found an unusual rock when he was out walking. It had a rough, sandy texture—in fact, it looked like sand that had been pressed together. What kind of rock did Steve find?**
   - Ⓐ igneous
   - Ⓑ crystalline
   - Ⓒ metamorphic
   - Ⓓ sedimentary

7. **Rocks are made of _____ .**
   - Ⓕ lava
   - Ⓖ fossils
   - Ⓗ minerals
   - Ⓙ chemicals

Directions: Read the question. Write your answer on the lines provided.

8. **What is the difference between sediment and sedimentary rock?**

_____

_____

STOP

Name_____ Date_____

Grade 4

Directions: Study the diagram below. Use it to help you answer question 1.

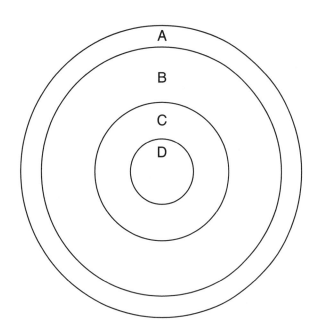

1. Write the name of the layer of the earth next to the letter representing it on the diagram.

   A. _____

   B. _____

   C. _____

   D. _____

Directions: Answer questions 2–4 with the name of one of the layers of the earth.

2. Which layer of the earth is the thickest?

   _____

3. Which layer of the earth is the thinnest?

   _____

4. Which layer of the earth do we live on?

   _____

Directions: Read the questions. Choose the truest possible answer. Shade in the circle before your choice.

5. What is the crust made of?
   - Ⓐ ice
   - Ⓑ rock
   - Ⓒ lave
   - Ⓓ water

6. What is the upper part of the mantle made of?
   - Ⓕ blue fire
   - Ⓖ tree sap
   - Ⓗ solid rock
   - Ⓙ liquid rock

STOP

0-7696-8064-X—*Science Test Practice*

Grade 4

Directions: Read the questions. Choose the truest possible answer. Shade in the circle before your choice.

1. **A plant's roots grow into the cracks of a rock, widening the cracks, and eventually splitting the rock. This is an example of:**

   Ⓐ erosion

   Ⓑ landslide

   Ⓒ deposition

   Ⓓ weathering

2. **What process creates sedimentary rocks?**

   Ⓕ erosion

   Ⓖ landslide

   Ⓗ deposition

   Ⓙ weathering

3. **Jung plants a garden in a corner of his yard. How will this prevent erosion from occurring on that plot of land?**

   Ⓐ Turning over the soil will remove rocks.

   Ⓑ The plants' roots will hold the soil in place.

   Ⓒ Moistening the soil will stop it from moving.

   Ⓓ Animals that visit the garden will move the soil.

Directions: Read the text below. Use information from it to help you answer question 4.

For years and years, the Colorado River flowed over the same section of rock. Slowly, the water wore through the rock, creating a long crack. Today, that crack is so long and deep that it is called the Grand Canyon.

4. **Did the creation of the Grand Canyon involve deposition, erosion, or weathering? Explain your answer.**

   _____

   _____

   _____

   _____

   _____

STOP

0-7696-8064-X—*Science Test Practice*

Name_____ Date_____

Directions: Read the text below. Use information from it to help you answer the questions.

    Landslides are a geological and environmental hazard as they can cause fatalities and property destruction, as well as billions of dollars of damage.

    Landslides are gravity flows of rock, the earth, and other debris on a slope, due to gravity. They can occur in connection with natural disasters or man-made causes such as over-development of hilly land.

Directions: Fill in the Cause and Effect Chart below. Be specific.

Cause	Effect
1. _____ →	
2. _____ →	A
3. _____ →	Landslide
4. _____ →	Occurs
5. _____ →	

Directions: Read each question. Write your answers on the lines provided.

6. **How can a wildfire cause a landslide?**

_____

_____

_____

7. **What is the difference between a landslide and a mudslide?**

_____

_____

_____

0-7696-8064-X—*Science Test Practice*

Grade 4

Directions: Study the diagram below. Use it to help you answer questions 1–2.

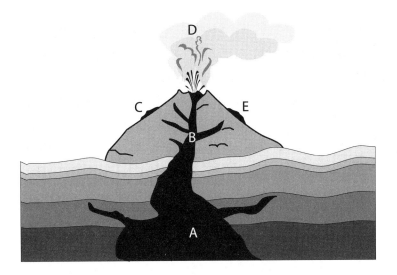

1. **What is happening at point E?**

   (A) Lava is flowing uphill and feeding into the volcano.

   (B) The pressure is building, pushing the magma upwards.

   (C) Lava is cooling, hardening, and becoming part of the land.

   (D) Material from the volcano is slowly disintegrating into the air.

2. **In what layer of the earth is point A?**

   (F) crust

   (G) mantle

   (H) inner core

   (J) outer core

Directions: Read each question. Write your answers on the lines provided.

3. **What is lava called when it is under the ground?**

   _____

4. **List three different types of volcanoes.**

   _____

   _____

5. **After a volcano erupts, what might a nearby forest look like?**

   _____

   _____

STOP

0-7696-8064-X—*Science Test Practice*

Grade 4

Directions: Read the text below. Use information from it to help you answer the questions.

When Tori's family moved to a new city, her dad made sure that she knew all about earthquakes. There had never been an earthquake in their old town, so Tori did not know what she should do. Her dad showed her how to drop to the floor and crawl under a table or desk. He told her to hold on to the leg of the table and protect her eyes with one arm.

About a week after Tori began her new school, her teacher made an announcement. "Today we are going to have an earthquake drill," she said. "That way we'll be prepared if an earthquake happens while we're in class. Does anybody know what you should do first if you feel the ground start to shake?"

Tori raised her hand high in the air. She knew exactly what to do!

1. **Tori's new city seems to be a place where earthquakes sometimes happen. Her new home is probably _____ .**

   (A) along a fault

   (B) near a volcano

   (C) in a crowded area

   (D) on the middle of a plate

2. **What causes the ground to shake during an earthquake?**

   _____

   _____

   _____

   _____

STOP

Name_____ Date_____

Directions: Study the diagram below. Use it to help you answer questions 1–3.

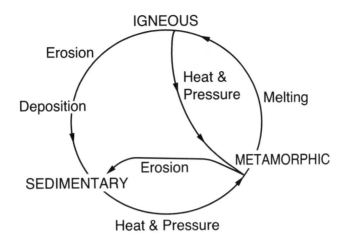

1. **What will happen if an igneous rock is put under a large amount of heat and pressure?**

   Ⓐ It will weather.

   Ⓑ It will melt into lava.

   Ⓒ It will become a sedimentary rock.

   Ⓓ It will become a metamorphic rock.

2. **An igneous rock is formed when another rock is _____ .**

   Ⓕ melted

   Ⓖ squeezed

   Ⓗ weathered

   Ⓙ compacted

3. **What must happen to metamorphic rock for it to become sedimentary rock?**

   _____

   _____

STOP

0-7696-8064-X—*Science Test Practice*

Grade 4

Directions: Based on what you know about the gases in air, fill in the blanks on the pie graph below.

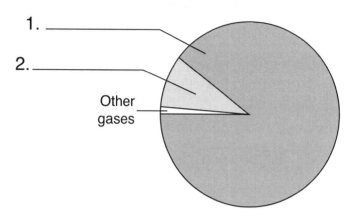

1. _____
2. _____

Other gases _____

Directions: Read the questions. Choose the truest possible answer. Shade in the circle before your choice.

3. **Rabbits, fish, and bluebirds all take in _____ in order to survive.**

   - Ⓐ oxygen
   - Ⓑ nitrogen
   - Ⓒ water vapor
   - Ⓓ carbon dioxide

4. **How does the atmosphere warm the earth?**

   - Ⓕ It sends out radioactive waves.
   - Ⓖ It produces high-temperature rays.
   - Ⓗ It combines with oxygen to create heat.
   - Ⓙ It keeps the sun's warmth from escaping.

Directions: Read each question. Write your answers on the lines provided.

5. **Contrast the way that plants and animals use carbon dioxide.**

   _____

   _____

6. **How and why does the air pressure change as you climb up a mountain?**

   _____

   _____

   _____

STOP

 0-7696-8064-X—Science Test Practice

Name _____   Date _____

Directions: Study the table below. Use it to help you answer questions 1–6.

Layers of the Atmosphere

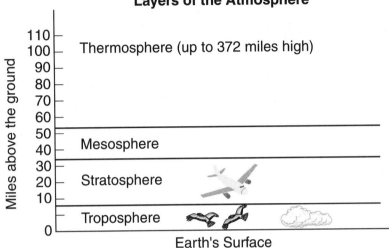

1. **Which layer of the atmosphere is closest to the earth?**
   - (A) stratosphere
   - (B) troposphere
   - (C) mesosphere
   - (D) thermosphere

2. **Which layer of the atmosphere is farthest from the earth?**
   - (F) stratosphere
   - (G) troposphere
   - (H) mesosphere
   - (J) thermosphere

3. **Julio is flying in a jet plane. Which layer of the atmosphere is he in?**
   - (A) stratosphere
   - (B) troposphere
   - (C) mesosphere
   - (D) thermosphere

4. **Which level of the atmosphere do birds fly in?**
   - (F) stratosphere
   - (G) troposphere
   - (H) mesosphere
   - (J) thermosphere

5. **The _____ is the coldest layer of the atmosphere.**
   - (A) stratosphere
   - (B) troposphere
   - (C) mesosphere
   - (D) thermosphere

6. **Weather occurs in the _____ .**
   - (F) stratosphere
   - (G) troposphere
   - (H) mesosphere
   - (J) thermosphere

STOP

0-7696-8064-X — *Science Test Practice*

Grade 4

Directions: Read the questions. Choose the truest possible answer. Shade in the circle before your choice.

1. **Tyrell lives in Florida, and the air is often filled with water vapor. The name scientists use to describe water vapor in the air _____ .**
   - (A) humidity
   - (B) temperature
   - (C) air pressure
   - (D) precipitation level

2. **When water vapor rises and condenses in the atmosphere, which of these forms?**
   - (F) clouds
   - (G) pockets
   - (H) sandstorms
   - (J) wind tunnels

3. **Water that falls from the sky is called _____ .**
   - (A) evaporation
   - (B) precipitation
   - (C) condensation
   - (D) maximization

4. **A hurricane is a large storm that _____ .**
   - (F) causes funnel clouds to form
   - (G) includes lightning and thunder
   - (H) forms over warm ocean water
   - (J) drops more than six inches of snow

Directions: Study the map below. Use it to help you answer questions 5–6.

5. **In which part of the country is there a high-pressure area, which indicates good weather?**
   - (A) northwest
   - (B) southwest
   - (C) southeast
   - (D) northeast

6. **When a warm air mass meets a cold air mass, what is formed?**
   - (F) a warm front
   - (G) a cold front
   - (H) an air mass
   - (J) a snowstorm

0-7696-8064-X—*Science Test Practice*

Name_____   Date_____

Grade 4

Directions: Match the type of cloud from the Word Bank with its description in the table.

```
┌─────────────────── Word Bank ───────────────────┐
│   Cumulonimbus   Cumulus   Cirrus   Stratus     │
└──────────────────────────────────────────────────┘
```

Type of Cloud	Description of Cloud
1. _____	thin, wispy high in the sky sign of fair weather
2. _____	dense very tall lead to thunderstorms
3. _____	solid sheet low in the sky may produce light drizzle
4. _____	flat bases and fluffy tops low in the sky sign of fair weather

Directions: Read each question. Write your answers on the lines provided.

5. **Li wants to have a picnic today. She looks up at the sky and sees very tall, dense clouds. Should she plan to have the picnic? Why?**

_____

_____

_____

6. **How do clouds form?**

_____

_____

_____

_____

STOP

0-7696-8064-X—Science Test Practice

Grade 4

Directions: Match the type of precipitation in the Word Bank with its description in the table.

```
┌──────────────── Word Bank ─────────────────┐
│         Snow    Hail    Rain    Sleet       │
└─────────────────────────────────────────────┘
```

Type of Precipitation	Description of Precipitation
1. _____	drops of frozen water melt as they fall
2. _____	drops of water freeze into ice while in a cloud
3. _____	drops of water fall, temperature above freezing
4. _____	drops of water vapor form ice crystals as they fall

Directions: Read the question. Choose the truest possible answer. Shade in the circle before your choice.

5. **If the temperature in a cloud is above freezing, what types of precipitation might fall from that cloud?**

   Ⓐ rain or snow
   Ⓑ rain or sleet
   Ⓒ sleet or hail
   Ⓓ sleet or snow

STOP

Name_____ Date_____

Directions: Study the diagram below. Use it to help you answer questions 1–6.

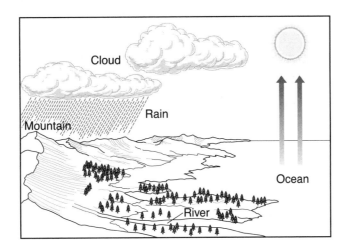

1. The rain falling on the mountain is a form of _____ .
   - Ⓐ cloud
   - Ⓑ precipitation
   - Ⓒ evaporation
   - Ⓓ condensation

2. Under the sun's warmth, the water in the ocean _____ .
   - Ⓕ runs off
   - Ⓖ sinks down
   - Ⓗ precipitates
   - Ⓙ evaporates

3. The rain on the mountain runs into the _____ and goes to the ocean.
   - Ⓐ sun
   - Ⓑ river
   - Ⓒ ocean
   - Ⓓ ground

4. This picture shows the _____ .
   - Ⓕ rock cycle
   - Ⓖ water cycle
   - Ⓗ rock system
   - Ⓙ water system

5. What forms does water go through in the water cycle?

   _____

   _____

   _____

6. What is condensation?

   _____

   _____

STOP

0-7696-8064-X—*Science Test Practice*

Grade 4

Directions: Read the text below. Use information from it to help you answer questions 1–3.

Most of the water on the earth is salty ocean water. Only about 3% of all the earth's water is fresh. Fresh water is stored as ice in giant glaciers that cover Antarctica and Greenland. A very small amount is found in rivers, streams, lakes, and ponds.

There is also water under the earth's surface. Called groundwater, it is an important source of water for many people.

1. **Where would you find salt water?**
   - (A) in a river
   - (B) in a glacier
   - (C) in an ocean
   - (D) underground

2. **Which statement about water is true?**
   - (F) Ponds hold about 3% of all water on the earth.
   - (G) No water exists beneath the surface of the earth.
   - (H) The earth has much more salt water than fresh water.
   - (J) Most of the earth's water is stored as ice in giant glaciers.

3. **Why must fresh water be conserved and used wisely?**
   - (A) because there is so little of it
   - (B) because there is so much of it
   - (C) because it is only found in rivers
   - (D) because we can use salty water instead

Directions: Study the chart to the right. Use it to help you answer question 4.

4. **What is the longest river in the United States?**
   - (F) Colorado River
   - (G) Yukon River
   - (H) Missouri River
   - (J) Mississippi River

Rivers of the United States	
Name of River	**Length of River**
Yukon	1,980 miles
Rio Grande	1,900 miles
Arkansas	1,460 miles
St. Lawrence	1,900 miles
Mississippi	2,340 miles
Colorado	1,450 miles
Missouri	2,540 miles

0-7696-8064-X—Science Test Practice

— Grade 4 —

Directions: Read the question. Choose the truest possible answer. Shade in the circle before your choice.

1. **Each day, twice a day, the sea reaches high up on the beach and then retreats. These daily motions are called _____ .**

   (A) tides

   (B) waves

   (C) currents

   (D) whirlpools

Directions: Study the diagram below. Use it to help you answer questions 2–5.

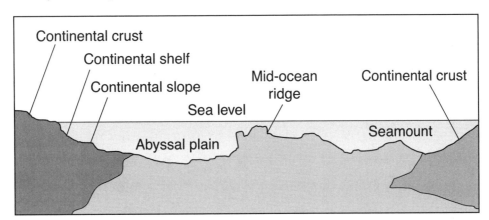

2. **What part of the sea floor is deepest?**

   (F) abyssal plain

   (G) continental shelf

   (H) mid-ocean ridge

   (J) continental crust

3. **Parts of the _____ can be above sea level.**

   (A) abyssal plain

   (B) mid-ocean ridge

   (C) continental shelf

   (D) continental crust

4. **Denisha went to the beach. Which of the following did she stand on?**

   (F) seamount

   (G) abyssal plain

   (H) mid-ocean ridge

   (J) continental shelf

5. **The ocean water is constantly moving around the world in great, river-like streams. What are these streams called?**

   (A) tides

   (B) waves

   (C) currents

   (D) whirlpools

0-7696-8064-X—*Science Test Practice*

Name_____ Date_____

Directions: Fill in the diagram of the sun below. Use the words from the Word Bank.

Word Bank

sunspot
solar flare

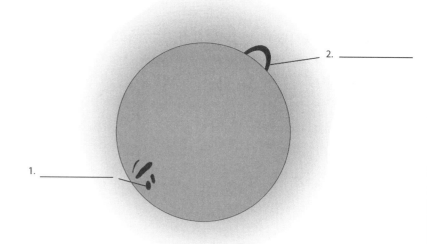

1. _____

2. _____

Directions: Read the questions. Choose the truest possible answer. Shade in the circle before your choice.

3. **What is the sun made of?**

   (A) gas

   (B) rock

   (C) electric current

   (D) magnetic energy

4. **The sun is a(n) _____ , so it makes its own light.**

   (F) star

   (G) orbit

   (H) moon

   (J) planet

Directions: Study the diagram below. Use it to help you answer questions 5–6.

The Sun and Other Stars			
Star	**Size**	**Color**	**Surface Temperature**
the sun	1.3 million km	yellow	6000°C
Aldebaran	13 million km	red	−178°C
Sirius	1.6 million km	yellow	27,200°C
Rigel	13.4 million km	blue	10,730°C

5. **Which of the stars in the chart has the highest temperature?**

   (A) sun

   (B) Rigel

   (C) Sirius

   (D) Aldebaran

6. **What color are the sun and Sirius?**

   (F) red

   (G) blue

   (H) green

   (J) yellow

84

Grade 4

Directions: Fill in the blanks on the diagram with the correct name of each planetary object from the Word Bank.

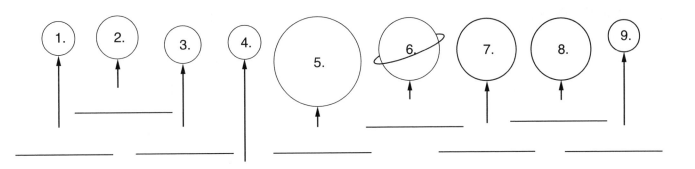

Word Bank

Venus   Mars   Earth   Mercury   Pluto

Neptune   Saturn   Jupiter   Uranus

Directions: Read each question. Write your answers on the lines provided.

10. **Compare and contrast the earth and Mars.**

_____

_____

_____

_____

_____

11. **Why can life survive on the earth but not on the other planets in our solar system?**

_____

_____

12. **What is the difference between a planetary object and a moon?**

_____

_____

STOP

0-7696-8064-X—*Science Test Practice*

Grade 4

Directions: Read the questions. Choose the truest possible answer. Shade in the circle before your choice.

1. **What is moonlight?**
   - Ⓐ reflected sunlight
   - Ⓑ burning oxygen
   - Ⓒ boiling atmosphere
   - Ⓓ evaporated methane

2. **The moon's craters were probably caused by _____ .**
   - Ⓕ atmospheric pressure
   - Ⓖ meteors that hit the moon
   - Ⓗ gases on the moon's surface
   - Ⓙ the lack of water on the moon

3. **Which of the following shows a picture of the proper lineup for a lunar eclipse?**

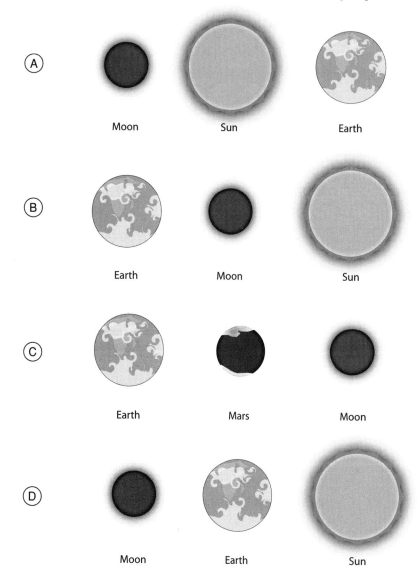

Ⓐ   Moon   Sun   Earth

Ⓑ   Earth   Moon   Sun

Ⓒ   Earth   Mars   Moon

Ⓓ   Moon   Earth   Sun

0-7696-8064-X—*Science Test Practice*

Grade 4

Directions: Read each question. Write your answers on the lines provided.

1. **The sun is an ordinary star, in terms of both its size and its brightness. Why does it seem so much bigger and brighter than other stars?**

   _____

   _____

   _____

2. **Show how the following words are related: the earth, Universe, solar system, galaxy.**

   _____

   _____

3. **Why can't you see stars during the day?**

   _____

   _____

Directions: Read the questions. Choose the truest possible answer. Shade in the circle before your choice.

4. **The _____ contains all of the matter in space.**
   - (F) Universe
   - (G) constellation
   - (H) solar system
   - (J) Milky Way galaxy

5. **A galaxy is _____ .**
   - (A) a group of millions or even billions of stars
   - (B) the cloud of gas and dust in which stars form
   - (C) a star that is much larger than the sun
   - (D) a star that is much brighter than the sun

6. **Jamie looked up at the sky one night and said, "Look, there's the constellation Leo!" What was Jamie looking at?**
   - (F) the tail of a comet
   - (G) a natural arrangement of stars
   - (H) an imaginary picture made up of stars
   - (J) a huge lion in the clouds

STOP

Grade 4 Posttest

Directions: Choose the truest answer for each question.

1. Jim thinks eating breakfast every morning will help him stay awake. He has not tested this idea out yet. It is his _____ .
   - (A) theory
   - (B) conclusion
   - (C) experiment
   - (D) hypothesis

2. _____ is an example of a natural resource.
   - (F) paper
   - (G) wood
   - (H) plastic
   - (J) cardboard

3. Matsu has a fever and is lying in bed. What does her fever show?
   - (A) Her body is trying to kill germs.
   - (B) Her stuffed nose is trapping heat.
   - (C) Her house is at a high temperature.
   - (D) Her medicine is not working correctly.

4. Eliana wants to know how long and wide her desk is. She should measure it with a _____ .
   - (F) ruler
   - (G) scale
   - (H) test tube
   - (J) thermometer

5. Robert's _____ would change if the force of gravity changed.
   - (A) mass
   - (B) height
   - (C) weight
   - (D) temperature

6. Since she learned about the importance of water, Anita takes shorter showers. She is trying to _____ water.
   - (F) waste
   - (G) reuse
   - (H) recycle
   - (J) conserve

7. Helen's finger might be about 5 _____ long.
   - (A) meters
   - (B) kilometers
   - (C) millimeters
   - (D) centimeters

GO ON

   0-7696-8064-X—*Science Test Practice*

Grade 4 Posttest

Directions: Choose the truest answer for each question.

8. **Molly's pet is hairy and warm–blooded. What type of animal is her pet?**
   - (A) a reptile
   - (B) a mammal
   - (C) an arthropod
   - (D) an amphibian

9. **Carol thought that the air around her was part of the earth. Her teacher told her it was actually part of the _____ .**
   - (F) earthsphere
   - (G) atmosphere
   - (H) water vapor
   - (J) oxygen layer

10. **Kamal puts a spoonful of jelly into a glass of water. The jelly sinks to the bottom because it has a greater _____ .**
    - (A) mass
    - (B) weight
    - (C) density
    - (D) volume

11. **In order to stay healthy, you must make sure to _____ .**
    - (F) eat all day long
    - (G) get enough sleep
    - (H) avoid eating any fat
    - (J) take many medicines

12. **Alex is holding a basketball. He is about to drop it. The ball has _____ energy.**
    - (A) light
    - (B) sound
    - (C) kinetic
    - (D) potential

13. **Daniela knows not to touch the radiator because it is hot. What kind of energy does it have?**
    - (F) light
    - (G) thermal
    - (H) potential
    - (J) electrical

14. **Mandy flips a switch, and a light bulb turns on. What kind of energy is at work?**
    - (A) light
    - (B) thermal
    - (C) potential
    - (D) electrical

15. **Liang is riding in his aunt's car. What should he do to make sure he stays safe?**
    - (F) wear a helmet
    - (G) close the windows
    - (H) buckle his seatbelt
    - (J) honk his aunt's horn

GO ON

0-7696-8064-X—*Science Test Practice*

Grade 4 Posttest

Directions: Write the truest answer for each question.

16. **Name one important safety rule for science experiments.**

_____

_____

17. **Which is more important to conserve: renewable or nonrenewable resources? Explain your answer.**

_____

_____

18. **Mary Jo had to answer a test question about ecosystems. She did not know what an ecosystem is. What is an ecosystem?**

_____

_____

_____

19. **How are earthquakes and volcanoes different?**

_____

_____

20. **Give an example of a liquid. How do you know it is a liquid?**

_____

_____

21. **Seasons change every year. How do animals survive with changing seasons?**

_____

22. **Halil has a compost heap near his house. He throws banana peels and moldy bread into it, but he does not throw plastic bottles into it. Why does he throw some things in and not others?**

_____

_____

GO ON

0-7696-8064-X—*Science Test Practice*

Grade 4 Posttest

Directions: Use the diagram to help you answer questions 23–25.

23. **Hakeem notices that puddles turn to ice when it is cold outside. This is his**

    _____ .

    (A) observation
    (B) hypothesis
    (C) experiment
    (D) conclusion

24. **Hakeem puts water in the freezer to see if it will turn to ice. This is his**

    _____ .

    (F) observation
    (G) hypothesis
    (H) experiment
    (J) conclusion

25. **Hakeem learns that cold temperatures turn water into ice. This is his**

    _____ .

    (A) observation
    (B) hypothesis
    (C) experiment
    (D) conclusion

Directions: Use the diagram below to answer questions 26–28.

27. **The bicycle in the middle has _____ energy.**

    (A) light
    (B) kinetic
    (C) thermal
    (D) potential

28. **Abby wants to know whether ice or wood is heavier. How might she figure that out? Include a hypothesis and an experiment.**

    _____

    _____

    _____

26. **The bicycle at the top has _____ energy.**

    (F) light
    (G) kinetic
    (H) hermal
    (J) potential

0-7696-8064-X—*Science Test Practice*

Page 9
1. C
2. H
3. C
4. H
5. D
6. F

Page 10
7. B
8. J
9. C
10. F
11. C

Page 11
12. D
13. J
14. A
15. G
16. D
17. G
18. D

Page 12
19. Lava is magma that is above the ground.
20. Jupiter, Saturn, Uranus, Neptune
21. The earth's gravitational pull is greater because it has more mass.
22. food, water, shelter, climate, and "to have young" (reproduce)
23. They protect soil from erosion, which allows that farmland to be used for a longer amount of time.

Page 13
24. C
25. parallel circuit, there are multiple paths for the charge to take
26. the two lights on the left

Page 14
27. I would advise him not to go on a picnic tomorrow, because there will probably be thunderstorms there.
28. A
29. The greenhouse effect is when heat from the sun is trapped inside of the atmosphere and warms the air.

Page 17
1. They were superstitious and thought lightning was a punishment for people who had done wrong.
2. Is lightning really a kind of electricity?
3. Answers will vary: Ben looked at lightning as something interesting to learn about. He might have found it scary, but he didn't let that stop him. He didn't agree with the superstition that lightning only hit those who had done wrong. He decided to use science and conduct an experiment to find out what lightning really was.
4. Answers will vary.

Page 18
1. D
2. G
3. A
4. G

Page 19
1. D
2. F
3. C
4. G
5. D
6. G

Page 20
1. C
2. H

Page 21
1. C
2. F
3. C
4. F

Page 23
1. D
2. F
3. The side of the balance with the inflated baloon should be lower than the side with the uninflated balloon.

Page 24
1. D
2. H
3. C
4. F

Page 25
1. D
2. J
3. B
4. F
5. C

Page 27
1. #1 is taller/bigger than #2
2. #1 is a cylinder/round, and #2 is a box/square
3. #1 is a lighter color/lighter gray than #2
4. The skunk is black and white, it is medium-sized, and it is long and fat.

Page 28
1. C
2. H
3. Rocks have greater density than feathers. It takes a lesser volume of rocks to equal a pound.

Page 29
1. It does not change.
2. It freezes, becoming solid ice.
3. It boils, becoming a gas.
4. It melts, becoming a liquid.
5. D
6. J

Page 30
1. 1
2. 5
3. 3
4. 7
5. 2
6. 6
7. 4
8. B

Page 31
1. B
2. sink
3. float
4. sink
5. float
6. float
7. float
8. sink
9. float
10. float
11. sink
12. float
13. sink
14. float
15. sink
16. sink

Page 32
1. A
2. G
3. D
4. J

Page 33
1. Answer may vary: trail mix
2. Answer may vary: air
3. Answer may vary: carbonated bubbles in soda
4. Answer may vary: oil and water
5. 10 X's should be placed evenly spaced throughout the water.

Page 34
1. A
2. potential
3. kinetic

4. sound
5. light
6. electrical

Page 35
1. B
2. F
3. B
4. G
5. A
6. White light contains all the colors and the prism refracts them.

Page 36
1. C
2. H
3. D
4. The particles in solids are close together and bump into each other often.
5. Reflection; sound waves bounce off an object like light bounces off a mirror
6. Waves; energy produced by vibrations

Page 37
1. A
2. F
3. C
4. The spoon's temperature has increased.
5. Answers include: heat from a stove; hot liquid heating a coffee mug

Page 38
1. D
2. J
3. D
4. F
5. B
6. Answers include: the television, an alarm clock
7. Answers may vary: getting socks out of the dryer; touching a doorknob after walking across the carpet

Page 39
1. D
2. H
3. B
4. A battery supplies power
5. The circuit is completed. This allows power to flow through the circuit.

Page 41
1. B
2. The two magnets repelled each other. This makes it feel like the

two magnets are pushing each other away.
3. The opposite poles of the magnets were close to each other. They became attracted to each other.
4. The earth is a magnet, and the compass has a magnet in it. The magnet in the compass is attracted to the North Pole of the earth.

Page 42
1. C
2. H
3. Inertia is the tendency of an object to stay at rest or stay in motion.
4. A change in motion will be greater if it receives a greater force.
5. Relative motion is the concept that the speed at which you are moving affects how you perceive other things to be moving.

Page 43
1. A
2. The masses of the objects and the distance between the objects determine the strength of gravity between two objects.
3. Mars is small than the earth and farther away from the sun.

Page 44
1. a pulley
2. The pulley makes it easier to lift heavy items because it changes mass to distance.
3. a lever
4. Answers include: as a seesaw

Page 46
1. C
2. J
3. D
4. H
5. A
6. H

Page 47
1. B
2. G
3. D
4. H
5. They classify animals to understand the relationships between them.

Page 48
1. C
2. G
3. C
4. Answers include: Similarities: warm–bloodedness, feathers, 2

wings, 2 legs, hatch from eggs; Differences: size, color, nesting habits, ability to fly

Page 49
1. B
2. J
3. D
4. H
5. Answers include: shell, antennae, number of legs
6. Answers may vary: The backbone supports the animal. The backbone allows for a more flexible skeleton.

Page 50
1. C
2. H
3. A
4. Answers may vary: answers should include a climate, water, food, or shelter for the living thing chosen.
5. They need air to breathe and stay alive.

Page 51
1. D
2. J
3. B
4. J
5. Most mammals leave their mothers when they can meet their own basic needs
6. turtles, frogs, snakes, and birds

Page 52
1. B
2. H
3. B
4. J
5. A
6. G
7. Mosses need water to seep through all of their cells.

Page 53
1. C
2. G
3. B
4. F
5. Plants use carbon dioxide. Animals use oxygen.

Page 54
1. Answers include: They fall to the ground. They blow in wind and float in water. They are carried by animals.
2. B
3. warmth, water, and air

0-7696-8064-X—*Science Test Practice*

4. The bee has spread seeds for the plant. The bee has helped the plant reproduce.
5. stamen
6. pistil
7. ovary

Page 55

1. B
2. F
3. Answers include: Like animals, plants go through a period of growth before they are fully formed. They eventually come out of their seeds, which is similar to birth. They grow, reproduce, die, and decompose.
4. Answers include: life cycle of a butterfly with the larva, pupa, and adult stages.

Page 56

1. B
2. H
3. C
4. J
5. Energy enters the soil when plants decompose.
6. Answers include: Living things: plants, insects, animals; Non–living things: rocks, soil, air.
7. Answers include: new organisms could bring new diseases to the ecosystem; new organisms can destroy the habitat.

Page 57

1. A
2. H
3. D
4. A habitat is a home or an environment that meets the needs of an organism.
5. Answers may vary: temperature, availability of food, comfort, shelter
6. Answers include: This species would survive best in a habitat that has cool weather, soft soil to dig in, and a lot of plants around.

Page 58

1. D
2. G
3. D
4. G
5. B
6. grass→grasshopper→ snakes→hawks

Page 59

1. D
2. H

3. Dead organisms decompose and add materials to the soil.
4. Answers may vary: If a force such as disease or a storm decreases the population in one area, it may not affect the members of the species living in other areas.
5. Answers may vary: Eat dolphin–safe tuna.

Page 60

1. B
2. H
3. A
4. J
5. C
6. Answers may vary: by chopping down trees to make goods, by killing rainforest animals

Page 61

1. D
2. F
3. An instinct is a behavior that an entire population, or gender within a population, has from birth.
4. The mouse will probably run away.
5. The cat is responding to the cold temperature.
6. Answers may vary: I get a blanket when I am cold.

Page 62

1. D
2. H
3. D
4. F
5. Answers may vary: pulling a hand away from something hot, shivering in the cold
6. Pain warns us that we are doing something dangerous.

Page 63

1. B
2. H
3. D
4. F
5. A
6. The rabbits will not be in as much danger of being eaten by snakes, so the population will increase.

Page 64

1. D
2. J
3. Answers will vary.

Page 65

1. B
2. J
3. A
4. H

5. It helps them to blend in with the snow so they can hunt without being seen.
6. Answers include: The long beak helps the toucan reach fruits.

Page 66

1. B
2. by observing fossils
3. the teeth
4. Plants lived here long ago.

Page 68

1. B
2. Wegener could not understand how similar animals could live on different parts of the continents. According to his theory, the animals all lived on one big continent. When the continent split apart, each animal lived on a different continent, but was still similar to other animals from its original continent.

Page 69

1. igneous rock
2. sedimentary rock
3. metamorphic rock
4. A
5. H
6. D
7. H
8. Sediment is small pieces of loose material, and sedimentary rock is formed from sediment that has been stuck together to form a solid rock.

Page 70

1.
   A. crust
   B. mantle
   C. outer core
   D. inner core
2. mantle
3. crust
4. crust
5. B
6. H

Page 71

1. D
2. H
3. B
4. It consisted of weathering, because the rock wore away. The sediment was also drawn away by the river, which happened through erosion. Deposition did not help to create the Grand Canyon.

0-7696-8064-X—*Science Test Practice*

Page 72
1. earthquake
2. volcanic eruption
3. heavy rain
4. sudden snow melt
5. wildfire
6. It can destroy all of the plants on a mountain. Since the plant roots are not there to hold everything in place, the soil and rocks may fall and start a landslide.
7. Possible answers could include land and development and hillside management, flood and erosion control, natural disaster intervention programs, etc.

Page 73
1. C
2. G
3. magma
4. shield, composite, and cinder cone volcanoes
5. Answers will vary: It would be covered in ash and smoke, trees would be destroyed.

Page 74
1. A
2. The pressure deep inside the earth builds up and finally causes the plates of the earth's crust to move.

Page 75
1. D
2. F
3. It must undergo weathering and be "glued" back together again.

Page 76
1. nitrogen
2. oxygen
3. A
4. J
5. Plants take in carbon dioxide, and animals breathe it out.
6. The air pressure decreases as you get higher. This happens because there are more air particles closer to the earth's surface, so there is more air pressure.

Page 77
1. B
2. J
3. A
4. G
5. C
6. G

Page 78
1. A
2. F
3. B
4. H
5. C
6. F

Page 79
1. Cirrus
2. Cumulonimbus
3. Stratus
4. Cumulus
5. No, because those are cumulonimbus clouds, which will probably lead to thunderstorms.
6. Water in the air condenses to form water vapor.

Page 80
1. Sleet
2. Hail
3. Rain
4. Snow
5. B

Page 81
1. B
2. J
3. B
4. G
5. Water changes from liquid to a gas and back to a liquid as it goes through the water cycle.
6. Condensation is tiny drops of water that form from the change of water vapor to liquid water.

Page 82
1. C
2. H
3. A
4. H

Page 83
1. A
2. F
3. D
4. J
5. C

Page 84
1. solar flare
2. sunspot
3. A
4. F
5. C
6. J

Page 85
1. Mercury
2. Venus
3. Earth
4. Mars
5. Jupiter
6. Saturn
7. Uranus
8. Neptune
9. Pluto
10. Answers include: Both Mars and the earth have two polar ice caps, volcanoes, and other landforms. They also both have weather and seasons, and they rotate at about the same speed. The surface of Mars is red, and the surface of the earth is various shades of brown. the earth can support life and Mars cannot. Mars's atmosphere is thinner than the earth's and pinkish in color. Unlike on the earth, there is no liquid water on Mars. The earth has one moon, and Mars has two.
11. The earth has the right temperature and gases to support life.
12. A planetary object orbits a star, and a moon orbits a planet or dwarf planet.

Page 86
1. A
2. G
3. D

Page 87
1. The sun is much closer to the earth than the other stars, so it seems brighter and larger.
2. The earth is part of a solar system, which is a part of a galaxy, which is a part of the Universe.
3. The sun's light is so bright that it overwhelms the light of the stars.
4. F
5. A
6. G

Posttest

Page 88
1. D
2. G
3. A
4. F
5. C
6. J
7. D

Page 89
8. B
9. G
10. C
11. G

0-7696-8064-X— *Science Test Practice*

12. D
13. G
14. D
15. H

Page 90

16. Answers include: wear safety goggles, don't taste anything unless told to by a teacher.
17. It is more important to conserve nonrenewable resources, because they cannot be replaced once they are used up.
18. An ecosystem is a place where groups of living things live together.
19. Earthquakes shake part of the earth. Volcanoes erupt from inside the earth.
20. Answers may vary: Water is a liquid because it takes the shape of its container.
21. They adapt to their environment, sometimes by migrating or hibernating.
22. Banana peels and moldy bread will disintegrate and replenish the soil. Plastic bottles take many thousands of years to disintegrate.

Page 91

23. A
24. H
25. D
26. J
27. B
28. Answers include: Abby's hypothesis could be that ice is heavier. She can use a scale to measure a piece of wood and an ice cube that are the same size and see whether her hypothesis is right.